WHAT PEOPLE ARE SAYING ABOUT SAM CHAND...

Sam Chand has dedicated his life to champion the success of others. Known as a "dream releaser," Sam is a leader of leaders who will constantly challenge and lift our mind-sets, self-imposed limitations, and unexamined choices. Sam writes from the enormous wealth of his own experience with uncanny insight, good humor, and pragmatic advice.

—*Brian Houston*
Global Senior Pastor, Hillsong Church

Sam Chand's teaching is a secret weapon resulting in the increase of effective materialization of your unrealized potential.

—*Bishop T. D. Jakes*
New York Times Best-Selling Author

Dr. Chand has been one of the most valuable mentors in my life and ministry. He has tremendous character, valuable leadership insight, a contagious sense of humor, and a pastor's heart. He has mentored me and made me a much stronger spiritual leader.

—*Craig Groeschel*
Senior Pastor, Life.Church

Samuel Chand is a leader's leader. His keen insights and vast leadership exposure have prepared him well for resourcing the kingdom. His natural passion for leadership development is a refined gift he enthusiastically shares with leaders and developing leaders.

—*John C. Maxwell*
Founder, EQUIP
New York Times Best-Selling Author

No one does this better than Sam Chand, and I can say that from our experience working with him in my own church. His reputation for helping companies find their way in the twenty-first century is exemplary and his integrity is beyond reproach.

—*Jentezen Franklin*
Senior Pastor, Free Chapel
New York Times Best-Selling Author

Great leaders have mastered the art of asking great questions, but legendary leaders like Sam Chand have mastered the art of questioning their own thinking.

—*Steven Furtick*
Founder and Lead Pastor, Elevation Church

Change is on the horizon, but it will not come by accident—it will require intentionality by those who lead the way! As a voice of influence on the subject of leadership, my friend Sam Chand will help you shape your future by reshaping the way you think!

—*John Bevere*
Best-Selling Author and Minister
Cofounder, Messenger International

One of the most respected voices on church and ministry leadership today is Dr. Sam Chand. On his website, his tag line is, "My life's vision is helping others succeed"—and he's good at it. Sam and I have shared a number of clients over the years, and time and time again, I've seen him turn around struggling churches, inspire frustrated leaders, and transform the culture at failing organizations.

—*Phil Cooke*
Media Producer and Consultant
Author, *The Way Back*

Sam Chand will expand your thinking, give you fresh tools, and help you navigate your leadership journey.

—*Mark Batterson*
Lead Pastor, National Community Church

Just when I thought my friend Sam Chand had reached his pinnacle, he transcends to a new dimension. Sam has a masterful skill of asking piercing questions, which are better questions that lead to better answers and ultimately a better life!

—Bishop Dale C. Bronner
Author/Founder, Word of Faith Family Worship
Cathedral

THE
SEQUENCE
TO
SUCCESS

*THREE O'S THAT WILL TAKE YOU
ANYWHERE IN LIFE*

SAMUEL R. CHAND

WHITAKER
HOUSE

THE SEQUENCE TO SUCCESS
Three O's That Will Take You Anywhere in Life

Samuel R. Chand Consulting
950 Eagle's Landing Parkway Suite 295
Stockbridge, GA 30281
www.samchand.com

ISBN: 978-1-64123-393-4 | eBook ISBN: 978-1-64123-392-7

Printed in the United States of America
© 2020 by Samuel R. Chand
All rights reserved.

Whitaker House
1030 Hunt Valley Circle | New Kensington, PA 15068
www.whitakerhouse.com

Library of Congress Cataloging-in-Publication Data
LC record available at https://lccn.loc.gov/2019053518
LC ebook record available at https://lccn.loc.gov/2019053519

1 2 3 4 5 6 7 8 9 10 11 ᏔᎯ 27 26 25 24 23 22 21 20

CONTENTS

Introduction: *How Did I Get Here?* 11

PART ONE: OBSERVATIONS

1. The Camera Is Always On
   What do they see? 21

2. Better Lenses
   When we look at others, what do we see? 45

PART TWO: OPINIONS

3. The Product of Opinions
   *Your life has been shaped by others' opinions
   of you* 67

4. Your Opinion Matters
   *Our conclusions have incredible power
   to change lives.* 87

PART THREE: OPPORTUNITIES

5. The People Standing at Our Doors
    They've given us opportunities. 109

6. Our Hands on Their Doors
    *Providing opportunities for the people
    around you*... 131

Conclusion: Continuous Improvement............................ 155

About the Author.. 167

INTRODUCTION
How Did I Get Here?

Have you ever wondered how you got where you are today—at this time, in this role, with these people, and with this purpose? I'm not only talking about the influence of your DNA and past generations of your family. I'm also referring to the mysterious series of interactions and events that have shaped your life. I think about this question all the time. It fascinates me because virtually all of us can trace our current situations back to three crucial engagements: someone *observed* us, formed a positive *opinion* of us, and then said, "I think you'd be good at... Let me give you this *opportunity*."

That's certainly my story. When I came to the United States from India in 1973, America was in the middle of an economic downturn. The recession wasn't just on the spreadsheets of economists; every person in the country felt the pain. The evening news often showed long lines at gas stations; soon, people could only buy gas every other day of the week. The cost of electricity was skyrocketing, so some states and cities recommended an "austere Christmas" without lights on trees or houses. The gloom became so oppressive that a radio station held a "Don't cancel Christmas" campaign.[1] The prime interest rate was three times higher than most mortgage rates today and many Americans were desperately looking for jobs. Immigrants like me couldn't get work permits because we would be taking jobs away from citizens.

I had come to America to go to college and not long after I started attending classes, the administration realized I had run out of money. They graciously allowed me to work as a breakfast cook and dishwasher in the mornings and as a janitor after classes in the afternoon. The administrators *observed* my need, formed a positive *opinion* of a struggling young man from India, and gave me an *opportunity* to work so I could stay in America and get an education. I graduated in 1977. Only twelve years later, after graduate studies and serving as a pastor, the college asked me to be their president. The board of trustees gave me an opportunity I couldn't have imagined a few years earlier as I cooked eggs

---

1. "Merry Christmas 1973," *Joe Moran's Blog,* http://joemoransblog.blogspot. com/2009/12/merry-christmas-1973.html.

and bacon, washed what seemed like a million dishes, and scrubbed floors.

To a great degree, all of us are the product of our families' input, our pleasant and painful experiences, promotions and demotions, awards and failures, good friends who believed in us and people who betrayed us, and countless other people who have whispered or shouted messages about our worth, our talent, and their visions of our future.

These three factors—observations, opinions, and opportunities— are verifiably sequential.

These three factors—observations, opinions, and opportunities—are verifiably sequential. People don't open doors for us unless they've first observed us and formed an opinion that we have the character and talent to step into the opportunity they can give us.

This isn't a one-way street. People have played this essential role in our lives and we play it in the lives of those around us. And no matter how skilled we've become, we can play these roles even better.

The sequence applies in business, the church, marriages, parenting, and friendships. It was even in operation when you picked up this book. Someone or something enabled you to observe that the book might be interesting, you formed an opinion that it's worth your time and money, and you're taking the opportunity to read it to see how it might add to your life.

I want to bring our subconscious assumptions into the light. We often assess others in the blink of an eye. We instinctively notice the look on someone's face, the tone of voice, or the body language that's consistent or different from the words being spoken. We react to our observation, but we seldom stop to analyze before we respond—it just happens and it happens immediately. We observe, form an opinion, and based on what we've determined in that second, we either give the person an opportunity to engage with us or we close the door and remain guarded.

Each part of this book contains two chapters. The first covers how others observed us, formed opinions about us, and gave us opportunities. The second describes the power of our own observations and opinions of the people around us, and how we can open doors of opportunity for them. This is a leadership book, but it's not limited to corporate presidents, CEOs, or lead pastors; it's for everyone who has a position of influence in another person's life—and that includes all of us.

With more insight and confidence,
you'll make better decisions to advance the people around you...
or perhaps show them to the door.

By the time you finish reading this book, you'll have the tools to be *conscious* of the three factors as you assess people. Your opinions will be more *consequential* because you'll give the right opportunities to the right people. With more insight and confidence, you'll make better decisions to advance the people around you...or perhaps show them to the door. These principles also help you become more conscious that people are observing *you* and forming opinions that will open or close doors of opportunity for you.

Every interaction makes a difference in your future and the future of the person you're talking to. And if we look long enough and closely enough, we might see something remarkable.

On April 11, 2009, on an episode of *Britain's Got Talent*, a frumpy forty-seven-year-old unemployed charity worker prepared to step on the stage. In her introduction, she explained that she lived alone with her beloved cat and she had never been kissed. Compared to the other contestants who were young and beautiful, Susan Boyle's television debut didn't look at all promising…until she started to sing. She walked to the center of the stage and sang "I Dreamed a Dream" from the musical *Les Miserables*. It was, by all accounts, one of the most stunning moments in the history of television. From the moment they heard her pitch-perfect voice, the three judges and the crowd shifted from scornful laughter to delighted wonder. After the performance, one of the judges, Amanda Holden, said what any honest person in the room should have said: "I am so thrilled because I know that everyone was against you. I honestly think we were all being very cynical and this is the biggest wake-up call ever. And I just want to say that it was a complete privilege listening to that."[2]

Susan Boyle became an overnight sensation, with invitations to appear on shows in the United States and Britain. Her debut album in 2009 set the British record for first-week sales and it was the second best-selling album in America.

Let me ask two questions: Who will notice your hidden talents? Who are the people around you waiting to be noticed?

---

2. "Odd duck to diva: How Susan Boyle became a star 10 years ago," Maeve McDermott, *USA Today*, April 11, 2019, https://www.usatoday.com/story/life/music/2019/04/11/susan-boyles-iconic-i-dreamed-dream-performance-turns-10/3426767002.

We must look at the lens through which we see the world, as well as the world we see,...the lens itself shapes how we interpret the world.

—Stephen R. Covey

PART ONE:
OBSERVATIONS

1

THE CAMERA IS ALWAYS ON
What do they see?

People are always watching you and me. Even when we're alone, the impression we've made on them is ruminating in their hearts and minds. Our spouse, children, friends, co-workers, bosses, customers, neighbors, teammates, and everyone else we encounter is forming opinions of us based on what they've seen in us and heard from us.

They notice:

...if we're insightful.

...if we're resistant to their ideas.

...if we're eager to push an agenda forward.

...if we're withdrawn or belligerent if we don't get our way.

…if we're always late.

…if we're constantly sharpening our skills.

…how we talk about other people.

…when we take the initiative.

Brenda and I got married after I graduated from college, and I took a job as the pastor of a small church in rural Michigan. I received a graduate degree and dove into my work to bring God's will to *"earth as it is in heaven."* During those years, the college trustees observed me and my wife as we served our church, sent students to the college, and supported its operation. This, I'm sure, helped them form an opinion that I was devoted to their goals and strategies. After several years, they asked me to join the board of trustees. When the position of president opened up and they began to consider who might fill the role, they turned to me. Their observations over those years gave them confidence that I was the right person for the job. They didn't tap me for this position when I was cooking scrambled eggs and mopping floors, and they didn't ask me to serve as president on the day I graduated.

In hundreds of moments for the next dozen years, the trustees noticed something in me. They saw that I was dedicated to the college and its purposes, and they knew that I had a high opinion of them. The board was convinced that I was a good communicator and I had earned the respect of leaders in our circles of influence. They were sure that I was a quick study—the learning curve might be steep, but they believed my ascent would be quick.

To be honest, I think they only saw me as a placeholder until they could find someone more qualified. I don't blame them. I didn't exactly have a sterling resume! But like many who are given an opportunity, I rose to the challenge. I became president in 1989 and I dove into my role with great enthusiasm. I wish I could say I was an instant success, but in the first two years, the number of students declined. That's not exactly what the trustees expected! At one point, the dean and I were driving to Nashville, Tennessee, for a meeting about accreditation. I turned to him and said, "Wouldn't it be wonderful if we had two hundred students?"

His eyes widened. "Sam, that would be incredible!"

At the time, *incredible* was the right word to use about this dream: it was hard to believe or scarcely credible.

Gradually, things turned around. When I became president, our college had eighty-seven students and wasn't accredited; when I left the college, we were fully accredited by two accrediting agencies and had more than eight hundred students. The success of my tenure surprised the dean and the board of trustees—and, to be honest, it surprised me, too!

DISRUPTION TESTS US

Each of us is where we are today because people saw something in us that gave them confidence in our character and skills. The camera was on us…and they were watching. Their belief in us may have come at a critical time when no one else believed in us—times of failure, times when we were on the shelf, or times when we had lost hope. We may have felt incompetent and unwanted, but somebody looked through the fog and saw our potential.

The observations made during times of disruption are much more significant than those during seasons of peace, success, and harmony. <u>More than ever, others are watching</u> <u>to see how we respond to criticism, obstacles, and failure.</u> In these times, they find out what's deep in our souls. <u>Like</u> <u>a tube of toothpaste, when we're squeezed hard enough,</u> <u>what's inside will come out for everyone to see.</u>

In times of difficulty and conflict, people tend to either get big or get little.

In times of difficulty and conflict, people tend to either *get big* or *get little*. Insecurity causes some to be loud and demanding, blaming others for their own mistakes and leaning forward to intimidate others into submission. That's *getting big*. But the same insecurity makes others wilt under the pressure; their voices become weak, they don't make eye contact, and they don't share opinions about anything because they're afraid of being wrong. They get so *little*, they almost vanish!

Do people notice if we're getting big or getting little? Of course they do! The people around us may be intimidated when we're loud and demanding. On the other hand, they may feel sorry for us when we've gotten so meek that we've almost vanished. However, either way, we lose their respect.

Times of disruption are the clearest lenses on who we are, what we're made of, and how much we can be trusted.

Times of disruption are the clearest lenses on who we are, what we're made of, and how much we can be trusted.

WHAT THEY SEE

Some aspects of our lives can be hidden behind a smile, but particular features are readily apparent—specifically attitude, preparation, understanding, and articulation.

Attitude

When I was president of the college, I walked into the office one day and greeted the receptionist. "Good morning! How are you today?"

She replied with a frown, "Oh, I'm making it."

I made a mental note of her response; I wondered if she might be struggling with something at home or at work. The next morning, I greeted her with a smile and asked, "How are you today?"

She slumped her shoulders and barely looked up as she moaned, "Oh, I'm here."

Of course, I noticed her demeanor. On the following day, I told her, "Good morning! I hope you're having a great day!"

She shook her head and said something similar to the previous two days.

It didn't take long for me to realize that if the college president was experiencing this kind of sour attitude, people on our staff, students, and guests were getting even worse! As soon as I sat at my desk, I called our business office.

"Please calculate what we owe my receptionist for her work through today and add another week's pay for severance," I told our chief financial officer. "Bring the check to my office and ask her to come in. Please find someone else to handle her duties while I meet with her."

A few minutes later, the CFO escorted her into my office and he handed me an envelope. I turned to her and said, "It's obvious you're not happy here. Here's a check for your work through today. We've added a week's pay for severance as you look for another job."

She was a competent person, but her attitude was corrosive to everyone who interacted with her.

People meet our attitude before they meet us. They see the expression on our faces from the first instant they look at us. In a split second, their observation turns into an opinion, which either opens or closes doors of opportunity. A good attitude is more than a smile. It's a can-do spirit, a genuine desire to be a positive influence in another person's life or on a team. It's not blind or superficial. It sees the truth and still believes the best of other people.

I'm always aware that first impressions are often lasting impressions, so it's important for me to set a positive tone in every encounter.

Preparation

When we walk into a meeting, do people see us with materials and resources we've prepared so we'll be ready to contribute to the discussion, or do they see us empty-handed—and too often empty-minded? We may assume *winging it* is fine, but people notice the level and consistency of our preparation. It's not just the boss who notices; everyone in the room realizes that we've done our homework…or not. They know that when we aren't ready to participate, we're just filling space in the room. And if we're the leader of the meeting, our lack of preparation wastes everyone's time.

I believe that preparation is one of the most important factors in determining a person's future in an organization. Failing to prepare once in a long while isn't a big deal, especially when there's a very good reason, but when people consistently aren't ready to dive into the agenda with researched facts and insights, they won't be on the list for the next promotion.

Preparation is one of the most important factors in determining a person's future in an organization.

I think about two questions: first, when I walk into a meeting, do people see me with materials I've prepared, my device in my hand so I can take notes, and any research I've gathered for the conversation? If they don't, they have every right to conclude that I'm not really into them. And second, after I give a talk, do I leave with the confidence I've given it my all, or do I know I should have spent a little (or a lot) more time making sure my points are rich, clear, and connected?

Understanding

When I meet with people, I want them to know that I *get* them. If it's a first meeting, I've done research into the person's background, studied the topic we're going to discuss, and learned about the person's family. I often find out more about them on a variety of media. My hope is that in the first five minutes of our conversation, the person will think, *Sam Chand really gets me!* When that happens, amazing things can occur. When I don't get enough information before we meet, I need to spend more time trying to get below the surface so I discern the person's hopes and dreams.

When I'm with Brenda, understanding is even more important. Do I come to those conversations preoccupied with my own goals and worries, or can I put those aside and be *all in* as I talk with her? If she has to say, "Sam, are you listening to me?" I know I'm in trouble! But when I listen patiently and invite her, "Tell me more about that," she knows I'm committed to enter her world and understand her heart's desires.

If someone asks me to fix a problem with their smartphone, I'm instantly sure he doesn't understand my vast technological limitations! The person doesn't get me. Understanding is a two-way street: I've become a student of the people around me so I understand what makes them tick, what they love and what they avoid, how they're motivated, and what drains them. As I understand them more fully, I can tailor my communication to be more encouraging or challenging, whichever is needed at the moment. Understanding isn't an add-on—it's essential.

Articulation

Communication is a vital ingredient in any form of leadership: in companies, in churches, and in families. In fact, we usually elect the politician who is the better communicator even if his or her platform isn't quite what we'd like it to be.

In private conversations, team meetings, small groups, and large events, people are watching me to see how I connect concepts with their hearts, if I can move them to take action, and if I'm giving them something they can use in the next hour or day. It's not merely the words we speak; nonverbal communication has an even greater impact than our words. Our facial expressions, tone of voice, gestures, and body language may correspond and confirm our words, but sometimes, they give a very different message.

In a *Forbes* article, Naz Beheshti observes that the first step is to become a student of our communication style:

Once we become more aware of our characteristic gestures and body language…we can then go about aligning our nonverbal signaling with our spoken message. This starts with clarity of intent. We think we know exactly what we want from a given meeting or presentation. In reality, however, our minds are often a jumble of emotions and random thoughts. If we take the time to hone in on the essence of our intention, then it is more likely to play itself out through our gestures, intonation, and facial expression.…This inside-out approach proceeds from emotion to gesture. Gesture sometimes anticipates and even shapes emotion and thought. We can choose to begin there and work outside-in. With practice, we can learn to be more conscious of certain gestures and nonverbal cues and, therefore, their effect on other and ourselves.[3]

Wise leaders pay attention to all aspects of how they communicate with others: in private meetings, small groups, and in large gatherings; online and in office memos; and verbally or nonverbally. Communication is as much art as science. We need to understand our audience, even if it's an audience of one. People need concepts, but they connect

3. "The Power of Mindful Nonverbal Communication," Naz Beheshti, *Forbes*, September 20, 2018, https://www.forbes.com/sites/nazbeheshti/2018/09/20/beyond-language-the-power-of-mindful-nonverbal-communication/#a94902d15018.

with stories we tell, so we need to use narrative to get our points across, even if the list of items on the agenda is long and time is short.

Even though I've been in the United States for more than forty years, I still speak with an accent. When I realize people don't understand what I'm saying, I speak more slowly and clearly. If that doesn't work, I use hand motions. Personal connections are so important that I'll do almost anything to be sure the person understands me.

PATTERNS SHOW UP OVER TIME

Most of what people observe about us happens instantaneously, but over time, people discern patterns in our behavior, patterns that tell them we're trustworthy or not. Trust is the glue of relationships. If we prove ourselves over many different experiences, people know they can rely on us, but if they see us cut corners or fudge numbers when we're under pressure, they have reason to wonder about our integrity. When we gossip about someone, we tell the listeners more than we probably want them to know about *us*... and they soon realize they could be our next targets!

People's observations about us may not be about our character but about our capacity in any given situation. They may realize we can handle a heavy load, or we may buckle under a certain kind of pressure. As they watch us for months or years, they observe our ability to persist

through thick and thin. Character and capacity—these tell OMG
people all they need to know about us.

ACT AS IF ALL EYES ARE ON YOU

In a letter to a friend, former U.S. President Thomas
Jefferson wrote:

> Whenever you are to do a thing, though it can
> never be known but to yourself, ask yourself how
> you would act were all the world looking at you, and
> act accordingly. Encourage all your virtuous dispo-
> sitions, and exercise them whenever an opportunity
> arises.[4]

Jefferson gave this advice two hundred years before
we had cameras covering every inch of stores and websites
tracking every click of a mouse. It's intuitively obvious that
we're on our best behavior when we know people are watching; today, people are watching far more than ever before.
Recent studies show that it doesn't even take human eyes
to improve our behavior. A group of British scientists found
that putting up posters of staring eyes had a similar effect.[5]
They recorded "littering behavior" in a university cafeteria

4. "The Letters of Thomas Jefferson," to Peter Carr, Paris, August 19, 1785,
http://avalon.law.yale.edu/18th_century/let31.asp.
5. "Effects of eye images on everyday cooperative behavior: a field
experiment," Max Ernest-Jones, Daniel Nettle, and Melissa Bateson, School
of Psychology, Newcastle University, May 6, 2010, https://www.staff.ncl.
ac.uk/daniel.nettle/ernestjonesnettlebateson.pdf.

and observed the number of people who threw away their trash instead of leaving it on the table.

> In their study, the researchers determined the effect of the eyes on individual behavior by controlling for several conditions (e.g. posters with a corresponding verbal text, without any text, male versus female faces, posters of something unrelated like flowers, etc). The posters were hung at eye-level and every day the location of each poster was randomly determined. The researchers found that during periods when the posters of eyes, instead of flowers, overlooked dthe diners, twice as many people cleaned up after themselves…. Humans (and other animals) have a dedicated neural architecture for detecting facial features, including the presence of eyes. This built-in system, also known as "gaze detection," served as an important evolutionary tool in ancestral environments (e.g. for detecting lurking enemies). Furthermore, the ability to function in social situations hinges on our ability to exploit social information provided by the expressions of the faces and eyes of others. What's interesting is that this system largely involves brain areas that are not under voluntary control.[6]

---

6. "How the Illusion of Being Observed Can Make You a Better Person: Even a poster with eyes on it changes how people behave," Sander van der Linden, *Scientific American*, May 3, 2011, https://www.scientificamerican.com/article/how-the-illusion-of-being-observed-can-make-you-better-person.

Many of us have given others far too much personal information on social media platforms. Our movements can be tracked through the GPS on our phones. Jefferson's advice was sound two centuries ago and, if anything, it's even more relevant today because we're almost always being observed by someone—or something. We're rarely really alone. Many companies use sophisticated software to monitor the effectiveness of their employees and track their progress. In these organizations, there are always *eyes* on us.[7]

COURAGE AND QUESTIONS

In the last few years, I've made it my practice to <u>invite people to tell me what they see in me.</u> I don't limit this inquiry to those I'm sure will only make affirming comments. I ask virtually everyone with whom I have meaningful interactions. I may ask:

- What do you need from me that I'm not giving you?

- How can I serve you better?

- What's helping and what's not?

Surprisingly, most people are thoughtful and honest in their answers and they have helped me enormously. Many years ago, I'm pretty sure I wouldn't have wanted to hear what some of these people would have told me, but as I've

7. "14 Best Tools to Measure Employee Performance," Scott Gerber, *Business.com*, February 22, 2017, https://www.business.com/articles/14-best-tools-to-measure-employee-performance.

become more, shall we say, seasoned, I'm not as afraid of the truth. In fact, I welcome it. Jesus came *"full of grace and **truth**"* (John 1:14). I'm convinced that people—myself included—can't hear the truth very well unless they experience the grace of love and acceptance. Then, their observations can become my truth, too.

When others see something in us that we can't see ourselves, their input can change the trajectory of our lives.

SOMETHING FROM NOTHING

Others' observations of us can be launching pads that propel us to places we never imagined we could go. When they see something in us that we can't see ourselves, their input can change the trajectory of our lives. We might conclude that our situations limit our potential because we don't have *the right people* helping us. Of course, a few people have advantages over the rest of us. Their families have enough money so they can attend the very best colleges and they have the right connections to open plenty of doors. We can look at them and feel resentment or self-pity, or we can realize that God has put people in our lives—perhaps people we wouldn't have expected—to observe us, form opinions of us, and open doors of opportunity for us.

The Scriptures tell us clearly and often that God observes absolutely everything in the universe, including us. We call this trait *omniscience*. For instance, the writer of Hebrews explains:

> *Nothing in all creation is hidden from God's sight. Everything is uncovered and laid bare before the eyes of him to whom we must give account.*   (Hebrews 4:13)

We sometimes read the Bible like it's a bunch of boring online articles and we miss the richness of the stories. When that happens, it helps to imagine ourselves *there*, at that time.

One of the most poignant passages in the Old Testament is found in Genesis 29 when Laban tricked Jacob into marrying both of his daughters, the gorgeous Rachel and the plain Leah. It was painfully obvious to Leah that her husband preferred *the other woman*, her sister. She longed to win Jacob's affection by providing sons for him. When she had her first child, Reuben, Leah said, *"It is because the Lord has seen my misery. Surely my husband will love me now"* (verse 32). The Lord saw the pain of her loneliness...but Jacob still didn't love her. Leah had a second son, Simeon, and said, *"Because the Lord heard that I am not loved, he gave me this one too"* (verse 33). But that didn't win Jacob over either.

Then Leah had a third son, Levi, and she hoped this would do it: "*Now at last my husband will become attached to me, because I have borne him three sons*" (verse 34). In that culture, a woman who gave her husband three sons was a hero! She would win the respect and admiration of everyone in the community, especially her husband.

Leah was sure God had *seen* the fact that she was unloved; He had *heard* her pleas for Jacob's affection and she hoped he would finally be *attached* to her. But even after Leah gave him three sons, Jacob still only had eyes for Rachel.

Then, something happened in Leah's heart. She realized that God's attention was more important than any man's, including her husband's. She had a fourth son, Judah, and this time, her prayer changed from desperation to contentment: "*This time I will praise the LORD*" (Genesis 29: 35). The fact that God—the Lord of love, peace, and strength—saw her was enough for Leah. Jacob didn't see her—but God did and He blessed her abundantly. It was through the line of Judah that He sent his Son to save the world.

When we put ourselves in the New Testament stories in the four Gospels, we see that Jesus had a way of surprising people. More than that, He frequently shocked them! His observations were often the opposite of what others saw—and that changed everything for the people He noticed. Pay attention to this moment:

*As Jesus went on from there, he **saw** a man named Matthew sitting at the tax collector's booth. "Follow me," he told him, and Matthew got up and followed him.*

(Matthew 9:9)

Jesus *saw* Matthew. The New Testament was first written in Greek, the language spoken all over the Roman world; in commerce, it was even more widely used than Latin. The Greek word translated "saw" is *theaomai*, which means "to behold, to view attentively." What did Jesus observe when He looked at Matthew? He saw a tax collector. In that culture, the job wasn't a respectable role like an IRS agent. In first century Palestine, a number of Jewish men collaborated with the Roman occupying forces to extort money from their countrymen. They were considered traitors, the scum of the earth. But when Jesus saw this despised man collecting taxes from other Jews, He saw something else, something deeper, something better. He looked beyond his treason and noticed two things: Matthew was good at his job and he had a heart for God. So Jesus called Matthew to follow Him. How do we know this is what Jesus saw? We look at the very next scene:

While Jesus was having dinner at Matthew's house, many tax collectors and sinners came and ate with him and his disciples. When the Pharisees saw this, they asked his disciples, "Why does your teacher eat with tax collectors and sinners?" On hearing this, Jesus said, "It

*is not the healthy who need a doctor, but the sick. But go
and learn what this means: 'I desire mercy, not sacrifice.'
For I have not come to call the righteous, but sinners."*

(Matthew 9:10–13)

This scene tells us that Matthew was open to the love
of Jesus, but we have another clue about his professional
expertise: he wrote the first book of the New Testament.
The gospel of Matthew was written to the Jews, Mark to
the Romans, Luke to the Greeks, and John to the believers
at large. It was crucial for the Jews to know the genealogy of
Jesus. Because Matthew was a professional accountant, he
began his gospel with the pedigree of Jesus: *"This is the genealogy of Jesus the Messiah the son of David, the son of Abraham"*
(Matthew 1:1). Then Matthew lists Jesus's ancestors to fill
in the gaps between Abraham and David, between David
and the exile to Babylon, and between the exile and Jesus.

Because Matthew understood Jewish culture from the
inside (as a Jew) and the outside (as a Roman collabora-
tor), his gospel is full of references to the Old Testament to
prove that Jesus is the Messiah promised by Israel's proph-
ets and it powerfully communicates the message of Jesus to
every reader, Jew or Gentile. When people open the New
Testament, they first read the account of Jesus's life written
by perhaps the most unlikely person to contribute to the
holy Scriptures.

Jesus caught flack for hanging out with people like Matthew. The religious establishment, the Pharisees, were fiercely loyal to the *law* of God, but they missed the *heart* of God. In the Gospel accounts, we often find them resisting and resenting Jesus because He saw value in people the Pharisees believed were worthless.

Matthew's story isn't an isolated incident. Jesus made a point of inviting Himself to lunch with a chief tax collector named Zacchaeus; He welcomed the gratitude of a woman of the night who found forgiveness and a new purpose in an encounter with Him; He went out of His way to explain His offer of *"living water"* to a Samaritan woman who was an outcast among her own people; He must have laughed with delight when four friends of a paralyzed man dug a hole in a neighbor's roof to lower him in front of Jesus; and He was amazed at the faith of a mother who badgered Him to cast a demon out of her daughter. Jesus's encounters with two sisters, Mary and Martha, were very different when their brother Lazarus died. When Martha went to Him, Jesus gave her a short seminar about the promise of resurrection, but when Mary fell weeping at His feet and other people wept with her, Jesus asked, *"Where have you laid him?"* (John 11:34)—and then He too wept.

Jesus observed intently and intentionally. He saw what others didn't see, especially in people who were considered to be traitors, outcasts, misfits, doubting, distraught, and "less than" in any other way.

By the middle of Jesus's ministry, He probably had seventy to a hundred people following Him. Luke tells us that Jesus spent all night in prayer and then chose the Twelve to be His apostles. The rest were still disciples, which means "followers," but Jesus picked twelve men specifically to carry the message after He was gone. Who were they? Most were businessmen who had skills and resources and chose to invest everything in their commitment to Jesus.

No matter what our backgrounds may be, people have had their eyes on us. They've noticed us, formed opinions of us, and have opened doors of opportunity for us. The first step, though, is always observation.

The camera is always on...and it's always on us.

Think About It:

+ Who saw your potential more clearly than you did at a critical point in your life?

+ How is your life different today because that person noticed something good in you? Connect with that person today to say, "Thank you."

The most beautiful people we have known are those who have known defeat, known suffering, known struggle, known loss, and have found their way out of the depths. These persons have an appreciation, a sensitivity, and an understanding of life that fills them with compassion, gentleness, and a deep loving concern. Beautiful people do not just happen.
   —Elisabeth Kübler-Ross, author and psychologist

The big challenge is to become all that you have the possibility of becoming. You cannot believe what it does to the human spirit to maximize your human potential and stretch yourself to the limit.
                    —Jim Rohn, entrepreneur and author

2

BETTER LENSES
When we look at others, what do we see?

Too often in my travels, my flight is cancelled. When this scenario occurs and I approach the agent at the desk to reschedule my flight, I can instantly read the person's mood: exasperation, boredom, annoyance, or glad to help by fixing the problem. Before I say a word, I've made an observation and formed an opinion so I can shape my inter-action to accomplish my goal of getting on the next available flight. If the agent is surly and I match his mood with angry demands, I've created an enemy instead of winning a friend. When I notice the agent isn't exactly excited to see me, I smile a little more, soften my voice a bit, and enter his world with a simple comment like, "I'm sure this is as hard on you as it is on us." This almost always elicits a smile and paves the way for a productive encounter. My initial observation shaped my response to the airline agent.

In the last chapter, we saw that disruption reveals our character; now, we notice how it reveals the character of those we're watching. We make the most accurate observations about people when we see them respond to stress. As leaders, parents, and friends, perhaps our greatest responsibility is to be students of people, to notice their character when they're under pressure and see how they use their intellect and talents to solve problems. This means our goal isn't always to relieve the pressure. People learn far more from facing difficulties than enjoying unbroken success. It's far more productive if we coach them to respond to the strains of life with wisdom and courage. Our observations shape our vision of the person, and with the opinions we draw from the responses to problems, we give greater opportunities or redirect the person's trajectory.

Reading people isn't limited to psychologists or those who are particularly gifted. All of us do it all day, every day...but we can always hone our observation skills a little more.

Sometimes, disruption in our lives takes us to a new level in our ability to make accurate observations. On March 5, 2018, Brenda and I were driving home at sunset on a two-lane highway when an oncoming car swerved into our lane and hit us head-on. Our SUV and the other driver's car were both traveling at about 45 miles an hour, so we collided at a combined speed of 90 mph. The front of our SUV was crushed. The airbags saved our lives, but Brenda and I had broken bones. As we waited on the side of the road for an ambulance, a policeman told us that the other driver had a blood alcohol level higher than the legal limit. I heard the words, but I'm not sure it mattered to me at that moment. My mind was totally consumed with Brenda's condition and my pain. We spent a night in the hospital emergency room getting checked out and rehab took several months.

There's something about this kind of event that heightens our awareness—we're more observant than ever before. Now, when I'm on a two-lane highway, especially at dusk, I watch the oncoming traffic like a hawk! When I pass an accident with an ambulance and a fire truck next to the crumpled cars, I say a prayer for the people involved because I know what they're going through. When I see the scene of an accident, I don't say, "That could have been me"—because it *was* me!

THE GRID OF EXPERIENCES

All of our observations are colored by previous experiences, which serve as a grid upon which we put what we see about people and events. Our backgrounds have trained us to notice certain things about people—and we're not as sharp to notice other things. Because I travel a lot, I notice people who don't travel much. They pack too much, they are impatient with the normal processes of flying, they're too loud, and they make a big deal out of nothing. But I also notice that the trip is often especially meaningful to them, which enables me to give them a bit more grace.

Our backgrounds have trained us to notice certain things about people—and we're not as sharp to notice other things.

For some people, observations are colored by past wounds of abuse, so they have become *hypervigilant*, on edge and watching for any sign of a threat, which they conclude could be any encounter. In this case, they have developed their observation skills to a high level, but their instant opinions of what they observe are clouded by the deep hurts they've endured.

Properly harnessed, fear heightens our ability to observe more accurately. When a child runs toward the street, the parents' fear gives them an adrenaline rush and the energy to run to grab the child before she gets hurt. This kind of fear subsides when the threat is over, but hypervigilant people never feel the threat is over. They're *always on*. However, when they experience enough love, understanding, and safety, they can learn to relax. They usually retain their incredible ability to read people and situations, but they no longer interpret everything as dangerous.

IT STARTS WITH YOU

Joe Navarro is a former FBI special agent and an expert on observational skills. In an article in *Psychology Today*, he explains that our observations may give us an intuition about someone and more observation will confirm or change our first impressions. Observations are the framework of our opinions. Navarro writes:

> It is never too late to start observing, but what do we observe for? First let's get some things clear about proper observation. Observation is not about being judgmental, it is not about good or bad, it is about seeing the world around you, about having situational awareness, and interpreting what it is that others are communicating both verbally and non-verbally. To observe is to see but also to understand and that requires listening to how you feel...[8]

When we notice how we feel around someone, we're tapping into our intuition. A *sixth sense* is often more accurate than what our eyes see and our ears hear. Does the person make us feel safe, understood, and believed in? Or

8. "Becoming a Great Observer," Joe Navarro, *Psychology Today*, January 2, 2012, https://www.psychologytoday.com/us/blog/spycatcher/201201/becoming-great-observer.

do we feel afraid, nervous, annoyed, suspicious, or belittled? Some of us are shrewd, but others are naïve. We're wise to pay attention to our intuition and at least do a little more observation before we make any kind of commitment. If we take the time to observe more fully, the effort is usually rewarded; if we don't, we often pay the steep price of being used instead of valued—and it may be very difficult to step back and disengage from the person.

THE DANCE OF DISHONESTY

Many people—including many leaders—are terrified that people will tell them what they really think about them. Maybe they've been unfairly attacked in the past, or perhaps simple misunderstandings have multiplied and caused deep hurts. They may smile, but they're as guarded as a medieval fort! They don't want anyone to find out about a particular flaw, a secret sin, or a past wound because they're too fragile to cope with exposure. When people get too close, they dance out of the way by changing the subject, offering a superficial explanation, or making excuses—anything to avoid feeling vulnerable!

And many of us participate in this dance by either avoiding the truth we see in others or using it to manipulate them to do what we want. We don't respect them enough to have honest conversations, or we're too afraid of what they might say about us. Love propels us to step in, to speak words of grace *and* truth—grace so that people can hear the truth. The purpose of perception isn't condemnation or manipulation. Accurate observation can be used like an ax or a scalpel, to harm or to heal.

WHY POWER

Every organization has a culture, ranging from toxic to inspiring.[9] We may not agree with every decision that's made by a leader, but we need to understand *why* the decisions were made. We can observe the goals—and the difference between stated and actual goals—as well as the values, vision, and relationships. Two organizations may have the same goal (their *what*), but they can have very different reasons for accomplishing it (their *why*).

As leaders, the only two strategic, big-picture questions are what and why. Every other question is tactical: how, who, where, how much, when, *and so on.*

---

9. For more on organizational culture, see my book, *Culture Catalyst: Seven Strategies to Bring Positive Change to Your Organization* (New Kensington, PA: Whitaker House, 2018).

As leaders, the only two strategic, big-picture questions are *what* and *why*. Every other question is tactical: *how, who, where, how much, when,* and so on. Outstanding leaders make sure they communicate the *why* of their organization clearly and often, and it's up to them to notice the employees who get it and those who don't. We can tell that a person understands the *why* by the type of questions they ask, the type of solutions they bring, their engagement in planning, and how they connect the dots between their work and the work of others. People who understand the *why* are more interested in the organization's success than their own achievements.

Grasping the *why* of the organization sifts out the extraneous from the crucial. For instance, if I'm driving home, turn the last corner, and see several fire trucks pumping water onto my house, which is engulfed in flames, I may realize there are some things I'd love to keep, but the risk of running into the house is too great. *Why should I risk my life for possessions that can be replaced?* Instead, I stand outside and think about *how much* will be covered by my homeowner's insurance. If, however, I drive up to my house and see the same scene, but I realize my child is inside, nothing in heaven or on earth will prevent me from running inside to save her. The answer to why I should run into the house changed, so my response to the situation changed.

Let me give some practical implications on how observations can make us better leaders:

Articulate the Why

When leaders are clear about the *why*, most of the people around them observe their focus and passion, and they get on board. Good leaders notice the ones who catch the vision and the rationale to accomplish the vision, and they give these people opportunities to excel. But these leaders also notice those who *don't* get it. They need to spend more time explaining the *why* and hope these people get up to speed. If not…

I've noticed that in some churches, many of the volunteers don't understand the *why* of what they do to serve. It's up to the pastor or team leader to explain that every person plays a crucial role in the church's effectiveness. Evangelism starts in the parking lot. If people feel welcomed by the smiling parking lot attendant, the gracious greeter at the door, the kind and attentive usher, and everyone else they come into contact with, they'll probably be more open to the message of the gospel. We can make assumptions that all of these volunteers understand the significance of their roles, but that would be a mistake. They're glad to serve, but they're far more engaged when they understand that the impact of the pastor's message depends, to some degree, on the warmth they communicate as people walk in the door. Every role is significant because they all have an impact on people, and again, first impressions are often lasting impressions. I've heard some people almost sneer, "I don't know why I'd ever go back to that church. Nobody even cared that I came." The people of the church, maybe including the pastor, didn't understand the *why* of their roles, so they didn't connect the church's purpose (and God's purpose) with what they do when they serve.

Of course, the principle of helping people understand the why is essential in every organization: churches, businesses, and non-profits. When people understand the underlying reasons for what they do every day, they put on clearer lenses, they see people more accurately, and they notice opportunities that have been there all along. With a clear why, people are inspired and energized; without it, they're disconnected—and often looking for the exit!

Look for People Who Bring Answers

Leaders need to hire and cultivate people who observe problems, but that's not enough. We also want them to bring solutions. When someone points out a problem to me, my instant response is, "So what do you think we should do about it?" I expect every person to be (or find) the solution to a problem. In fact, I ask them to present me with three options. Why three? Because the first two are often obvious, but the third requires deeper thought.

Think Creatively

In different kinds of organizations all over the world, I've noticed two kinds of people: those who ask, "What *is…?*" and those who ask, "What *if…?*" <u>Many people are focused on the present, the status quo, but others dream about what might be.</u> I love to interact with people who have nimble minds and are always considering possibilities. All of their ideas don't work out, but enough do to inject energy and passion into their organizations.

In different kinds of organizations all over the world, I've noticed two kinds of people: those who ask, "What is*…?" and those who ask, "What* if*…?"*

Winston Churchill was the prime minister of England during the darkest days of World War II, when his country stood alone against Nazi aggression in Europe. He could have wilted under the intense pressure, but instead, he gathered the brightest, most creative people around him, and together, they came up with dozens of innovative ideas. Many of them were complete flops, but some that seemed outlandish when they were first presented became crucial pieces of the Allied military machine. Churchill valued these people for their "corkscrew thinking." In an article for the British newspaper, *The Guardian*, Neil Finnie describes his approach:

During the second world war Winston Churchill declared a need for corkscrew thinkers—people with the ability to break away from the traditional linear way of thinking.… What followed was the creation of a number of special divisions. Alan Turing headed up the group who cracked the enigma code. Another counter-intelligence team devised the famous Operation Mincemeat. And the Special Operations Executive controlled a number of covert resistance units that would have been activated if Germany had invaded Britain. The department was unofficially known as the Ministry of Ungentlemanly Warfare or Churchill's Secret Army.[10]

Churchill and his little team of dreamers looked at the hard realities of *what is*, but they always moved to consider *what if*.

Value Stability and Trust

Trust is a hard-won commodity in every organization and we don't take it for granted. We observe the stability and constancy of the people on our teams, and gradually, our trust in them grows. Some people have great ideas, but

10. "Corkscrew thinking won the war. Here's how to use it in business," Neil Finnie, *The Guardian*, April 7, 2017, https://www.theguardian.com/small-business-network/2017/apr/07/corkscrew-thinking-world-war-two-business-winston-churchill.

they seldom follow through to make them a reality. Others are plodders who do their jobs with no flash or fanfare. We may go to the first people for creative input, but we go to the others to make them happen. We look for people who are predictable in giving all they've got to the team and the organization—but predictable in a good way. Trust is a feeling created by the reality of repeated proficiency. Trust is shattered by cruelty and unrealistic demands, it is gradually eroded by passive-aggressive behavior and passivity, and it is built by consistent respect and productivity.

Organizations can only go as far as the trust level of the leadership team. If the leaders have confidence in each other, they don't waste time guarding their turf. They can invest more of their energies in the goals of the team.

Some people have had painful experiences of having their trust betrayed, so they require others to earn their trust through unrealistic levels of performance—which never happens. These people always feel like victims because nobody can meet their standards.

We need a more realistic view of humanity: All of us are a blend of good and bad, right and wrong. As we observe people, we need to remember that wrong doesn't always mean bad, and right doesn't always mean good. A person can do something wrong and still be a good person, and he can be right and still be a jerk. We're multidimensional, complex creatures, not cardboard cutouts, so avoid quick, decisive labels that brand people as heroes or villains. Every hero has flaws and some really bad people may have some good ideas.

THE NECESSITY OF FEEDBACK

One of the very best ways to sharpen our observations is to get feedback from the people we're observing. But there's a problem: to some degree, most of us are plagued by *confirmation bias*—that is, we look for and listen to only the information that confirms what we already believe. In other words, we're not very open to differing opinions. Of course, some concepts aren't negotiable because they shape our deepest beliefs and form our identity, but many of our ideas could benefit by being challenged from time to time. For leaders, this challenge often takes the form of feedback. If we don't want it, it's only because we're not open to perspectives that are different from the ones we already hold.

A *Forbes* article explains the necessity of feedback...but only the right kind:

> Most managers understand the importance of collecting feedback on their performance and the organization in general from employees. In fact, a Gallup study of 469 business units found that managers who received feedback on their strengths showed 8.9% greater profitability post-intervention.

The trick, however, is to ensure you're getting *honest* feedback. Sometimes employees are afraid to criticize their manager or the company for fear of repercussions. Changing this perception—or better yet, preventing it from forming in the first place— requires building a culture of trust and transparency where all types of constructive feedback are encouraged, no matter the source.[11]

In the same article, leadership coaches were asked to give their best suggestions on how to get accurate and honest feedback. David Taylor-Klaus of DTK Coaching recommends: "Schedule two one-on-one conversations. In the first, ask only these three questions: What are you getting from me that you want more of? What are you getting from me that you want less of? What are you not getting from me that you want? In response, you only ask clarifying questions—no explaining or defending! In the second conversation, communicate what you heard and map out the changes and actions to which you are committing."[12]

And Jill Hauwiller of Leadership Refinery suggests: "I highly recommend leaders employ a 'skip-level' process for gathering feedback, where they meet with individuals two

11. "Want Honest Feedback from Employees? 16 Strategies to Try," Forbes Coaches Council, *Forbes*, October 17, 2017, https://www.forbes.com/sites/forbescoachescouncil/2017/10/17/want-honest-feedback-from-employees-16-strategies-to-try/#1fc904e929ac.
12. Ibid.

levels below them on a regular basis. As trust and rapport build, leaders can get incredible insights on what is and isn't working within their organization. This works for organizations of any size, so long as leaders remain authentically curious."[13]

As you can tell, the process of getting feedback takes time. We have to assess whether a more accurate and fuller observation of what's going on in the organization is worth the investment of time. Let me answer for you: It is! If we invest the time, we'll see our people and processes more clearly. We'll probably realize that at least some of our assumptions were wrong and we have the opportunity to make meaningful changes. Listening to our people usually earns their respect, even if we don't do everything they suggest. When they feel known and understood, trust is built, communication flows more easily, obstacles are overcome, and the organization grows.

DEVELOPING SKILLS OF OBSERVATION

Each of us can develop skills to observe the people around us. No matter how intuitive you may be, let me offer some practical advice:

Look for Clues

As you interact with people, don't think about the next thing you want to say. Train yourself—maybe by writing it

Major

13. Ibid.

in your notes in a few places—to make observations about
the person's body language, tone of voice, and facial expressions. Note any disconnect between the words spoken and
the nonverbal messages. Turn the camera on and keep it
on.

Ask Second and Third Questions

We usually learn much more when we ask follow-up
questions. The answer to the first one may be rote or superficial, but when we probe a little, we often get much more
information. Don't assume the person's first answer is the
complete answer. There's almost always more to explore.

"Tell Me More"

One of the very best statements you can make to get a
broader and deeper explanation is to simply say, "Tell me
more about that." It's conversation gold!

No Feedback Tells You a Lot

When someone refuses to engage in a conversation, or
engages only at a superficial level, they're telling you that
they're afraid to be honest with you. The problem may be
you, or it may be the other person. At the right point, stop
and say, "Here's what I think is going on right now. For some
reason, you don't feel comfortable talking with me. Would
you tell me if you see it this way too?"

Don't Expect Complete Alignment

People come from different backgrounds and experiences, with different perspectives on virtually every aspect of life. Learn to value variety, as long as there's alignment with the most important goals and procedures in the organization.

A KEY QUESTION

As I speak and meet with leaders, I ask them, "If you relocated your business or ministry two thousand miles away and you could take five people with you, who would you take—not counting your family?" This is a fascinating exercise. Quite often, leaders immediately think about the roles they'll need in their new venture: CFO, managers, youth leaders, marketing experts, and so on. When they head in that direction, I tell them, "You can always hire talent. I want you to pick individuals you trust and respect, people who add value to your life." They can often think of two or three, and then they get stumped. If their spouse is in the room, the spouse's list is usually very different from the leader's!

When they have finally identified five people, I ask, "What are you doing now to build into them? How are you investing in their development? Are you only giving them specific tasks, or are you doing life with them so they catch your vision and your heart?"

This exercise forces them to be more observant of their top people, the people who really matter, and craft a plan to help them become more effective—now and no matter what the future may hold.

The best leaders, parents, and friends are those who are skilled at observing others. No matter how proficient you think your skill is, don't take it for granted because you can always improve.

Think About It:

+ What is one practical suggestion from this chapter that you want to apply today? What difference will it make?

+ What are your regular, effective methods for getting good feedback from those around you? Do you need to make any changes to either get more accurate feedback or be more open to what people tell you? If so, what are the changes?

+ If you relocated your business or ministry two thousand miles away and you could take five people with you, who would you take, not counting your family? What are you doing now to build into them?

Great Quote

When people rely on surface appearances...rather than in-depth knowledge of others at the level of the heart, mind and spirit, their ability to assess and understand people accurately is compromised.

—James A. Forbes

PART TWO
OPINIONS

3

THE PRODUCT OF OPINIONS
Your life has been shaped by others'
opinions of you.

When I came to America in 1973, my accent was very strong. Quite often, people couldn't understand what I was saying. They tried, but after a few attempts, they shook their heads and tuned me out. It wasn't their fault; it was entirely mine. Immediately, I concluded that I had to learn to speak more clearly so people could understand me. After only three days in this country, I realized my name is unpronounceable to Americans. It's spelled Chand, but in India, it's pronounced Chunthe. Every time I introduced myself, people grimaced and asked me to repeat myself…again and again. I said, "I'm Sam Chunthe," and they said, "Chand?" I told them, "No, it's Chunthe," and they said, "Okay, I get it:

Chand." I quickly realized that if nobody in America could understand me, I needed to make a change. I didn't want to spend the rest of my time in the country laboriously correcting how people pronounced my name. That's how I became Sam Chand after three frustrating days.

The change has solved a lot of problems in America, but it created some far from here. I make regular trips back to India and when I introduce myself as Sam Chand, the people there look at me like the Americans did during those three days. They say, "Chand? Don't you mean Chunthe?"

"Yes, yes," I quickly tell them. "You're right. That's my name."

The pronunciation of my name was the first time people in this country misunderstood me, but it wasn't the last.

In 1979, Brenda and I wanted to get married and I made an appointment to ask our pastor to officiate. I was excited that everything was coming together for a beautiful wedding at the church. I'm sure he knew the purpose for our meeting and he was ready—but as it turned out, I wasn't. He turned me down. He told me bluntly, "I don't believe it will work for an American lady to marry a man from India. Mixed race marriages, especially in the South, have an uphill climb, and I want to spare you the heartache you would experience. Your marriage is almost certain to fail under all the stress."

I was surprised, but not shocked. Instantly, I thought about our involvement in his church: both of us were members, both of us tithed, both of us served faithfully, both of us were active in outreaches into the community, and both of us had very good relationships with the pastor and the people in the church. Before our meeting, I couldn't see any possible roadblocks. But I was wrong.

I could tell he wasn't going to budge from his opinion, so I didn't argue with him. But like all couples in love, Brenda and I were sure our marriage would last. After gathering my thoughts for a few seconds, I asked, "Well, then, can we get married in the church if we can find someone qualified to perform the ceremony?"

He must have anticipated my question because he immediately responded, "Yes, but there are two conditions: you'll need to rent the church for the wedding and I want to approve the person who will perform the wedding."

I agreed to his requirements. I asked another ordained minister to marry us and he agreed. I went back to our pastor to tell him our choice and he gave his approval. He charged us to rent the church for our wedding. As I write this chapter, Brenda and I are celebrating our fortieth anniversary.

A few years later, when Brenda and I served as pastors at a church in Michigan, I invited the pastor who turned us down to come and preach. He and his wife stayed at our home. By that time, our daughters Rachel and Debbie had been born. Brenda and I were happily married and serving successfully at a church and our little girls were thriving. Our church was strong enough to pay for the travel for this pastor and his wife and we paid him an honorarium for speaking. Neither Brenda nor I said, "I told you so!" but the scenes of our family life told him that his opinion of us had been misguided.

POWERFUL EFFECTS

A few people insist that they don't care about anyone's opinion of them. That's absurd. God has made us relational creatures. We live and die by the opinions of those around us. The question is: whose opinion matters the most?

We live and die by others' opinions, but the question is: whose opinion matters the most?

On three different occasions, Jesus—and those around Him—heard the Father's opinion of His beloved Son. At His baptism, the Father said, *"This is my Son, whom I love; with him I am well pleased"* (Matthew 3:17). At the transfiguration, as Peter, James, and John saw Jesus's appearance change before their eyes, they heard the Father say, *"This is my Son, whom I love; with him I am well pleased. Listen to him!*" (Matthew 17:5). And as Jesus arrived in Jerusalem for the Passover, when He would become the slain Lamb of God, some Greeks wanted to meet Him. Jesus told them that the hour had come for the Father to glorify His name. Then a voice that sounded like thunder came from heaven, saying, "*I have glorified it, and will glorify it again*" (John 12:28). The Father's opinion was paramount to Jesus.

Even Jesus, whose sense of security with the Father was complete and strong, was concerned about what people thought of Him. Ultimately, it was the opinions of the religious rulers that condemned Him and sent Him to the cross. Long before that day, Matthew tells us about a conversation between Jesus and His closest followers:

> *When Jesus came to the region of Caesarea Philippi, he asked his disciples, "Who do people say the Son of Man is?" They replied, "Some say John the Baptist; others say Elijah; and still others, Jeremiah or one of the prophets." "But what about you?" he asked. "Who do you say I am?" Simon Peter answered, "You are the Messiah, the Son of the living God." Jesus replied, "Blessed are you, Simon son of Jonah, for this was not revealed to you by flesh and blood, but by my Father in heaven."*
>
> (Matthew 16:13–17)

For Jesus, everything depended on people coming to the right conclusions about Him. If they formed inaccurate opinions, their futures were in peril; if they were right, they could experience the forgiveness, acceptance, and power He offers to those who believe. One way to read the Gospels is to perceive people's opinions of Jesus in every encounter. We find that some despised Him, some feared Him, and some adored Him, but nobody walked away from Jesus with a lukewarm opinion, saying, "Yeah, He's okay, but I wouldn't make a big deal about Him."

If *Jesus* cared about people's opinions of Him, it's important for *us* to understand the power of others' opinions as well.

HOW HIGH OPINIONS MAKE US FEEL

When people know us and have a high opinion of us, we feel:

Supported

We don't feel the pressure to prove ourselves. Instead, we feel valued and free to try almost anything. When we fail, we're not crushed. Instead, we learn from our mistakes. When we know we're safe, we don't try to hide who we are. We aren't always worried that we won't measure up, so we aren't constantly on edge, trying to earn a good opinion. One expert observed that when we're insecure, we're always in the courtroom trying to defend ourselves from the accusers (other people or our own thoughts) that condemn us.

The good opinion of people we respect inspires us to do our very best.

Inspired

The good opinion of people we respect inspires us to do our very best. Because they believe in us, we reach higher and attempt to do more—not to win approval, but because we already have it and we want to be worthy of it. Many people have told me that my books have had an impact on them, but none have been more sobering than the pastor who told me he had planned to commit suicide, but when he read my book *Leadership Pain*, he felt understood and encouraged. His comment inspires me to pour myself into every word in my books and speeches. When business executives, leading pastors, or denominational leaders not only invite me to give them input, but invite me back because they're convinced I've added to their leadership, I'm inspired to study hard so I can give more to them.

Resourced

When I feel someone values me, the two-way respect opens channels of communication so we ask each other for advice and other resources. The give-and-take of information and tools benefits both of us.

I appreciate it when people ask me penetrating questions. If they hear my advice as a consultant, listen to me speak at an event, or read one of my books, some people ask me to clarify a point or help them apply a concept to their specific situations. Sometimes, I ask them questions about what stood out to them and helped them. I want to know how the message I'm communicating rings true for them and I want to know if anything is confusing or irrelevant. I don't mind asking for their input, and usually, people are eager to be honest with me. Each of these conversations sharpens me and makes me better.

Challenged

When people have a high opinion of me, I feel challenged to live up to their high standard; when people have a low opinion of me, I feel challenged to change their minds. Either way, I'm committed to improvement.

Fear

My opinion of others calibrates my openness to their opinion of me. For instance, if I've given a talk and someone comes up afterwards and says, "Sam, you didn't make your points very clear. And besides, I don't agree with the ones I understood," I listen very carefully and try to assess the validity of the comments. I have to evaluate the person's feedback based on my opinion of its accuracy. But if Brenda tells me the same thing, I don't need to do any assessment because I already know she's right!

Unsurprisingly, the most significant criterion that determines my level of guardedness or openness to criticism is my respect for the person. If I sense the person genuinely cares for me, like Brenda, I may not like what I hear, but I take it very seriously. I'm convinced Brenda genuinely wants to help me be my best, so I listen very carefully when she says something like, "Sam, your second point wasn't as clear as it could be. Work on that a little bit for next time," or "It seemed that you were struggling to bring everything together at the end. Work on it and try it out on me before you give this talk again. I'll be glad to help." But if I believe the person is just venting and wants to exercise some kind of power through intimidation, I'll be polite and thank them for their feedback, but I dismiss what they say to me. All opinions are valuable, but some are far more valuable than others. I can tell when a person genuinely wants me to grow and excel.

All opinions are valuable,
but some are far more valuable than others.

RESPONDING TO CRITICISM

Most of us react defensively when people criticize us—even when the criticism is warranted and the person has our best interests in mind. In an article in *Forbes*, Nicole Lindsay shares her instant reaction to criticism:

> I've always envied people who can graciously accept constructive criticism. It seems I was not born with that trait, and throughout my career I've struggled with receiving feedback, even when it was entirely accurate. At the moment I hear the words of critique, my heartbeat quickens and my mind begins to race—first in search of an explanation for this assault on my person and then for a retort to rationalize whatever actions are in question.[14]

14. "Taking Constructive Criticism Like a Champ," Nicole Lindsay, *Forbes*, November 7, 2012, https://www.forbes.com/sites/dailymuse/2012/11/07/taking-constructive-criticism-like-a-champ/#4b4c10612c0c.

She makes several suggestions that change our mind-set so we can receive criticism without overreacting:

* In the first moment, watch your reaction and change it. We're tempted or compelled to be instantly defensive. Stop, take a deep breath, relax your face, and soften your tone of voice.

* Remember that honest feedback leads to growth. You may not want to hear it, but constructive criticism is often fuel for the future.

* Engage in dialogue. Our natural reaction is to discount the person's opinion and come up with dozens of reasons why he's wrong. Fight that. Instead, repeat back what the person is saying so both of you understand that you got the message. Ask clarifying questions, but without an edge to your voice. If you need to take another deep breath, do so. And use those magical words, "Tell me more about what you're thinking." Let the initial adrenaline rush and fight-or-flight reaction subside so you can listen, clarify, and have a meaningful conversation.

* Welcome the next steps. This conversation almost certainly isn't the end; it's just the beginning. You can thank the person for speaking with you and listening as you explained or clarified your perceptions. Set a time, maybe in a few days or a week, to talk again to be sure

you've made the suggested changes or ask additional questions.[15]

These behaviors don't come naturally to most of us. We have to fight against our conditioned responses to be defensive and redirect the blame to someone else, anyone else. These responses take practice, but if you spend time around people in any meaningful capacity, you'll have plenty of opportunities to hone these skills.

SNEAKING UP ON YOU

Sometimes, people form opinions of us that we didn't expect...and perhaps didn't want. It's helpful to understand how their opinions are formed.

Opinions Are Instant Analysis

In every encounter, our observations are interpreted through the grid of past experiences in the blink of an eye. Well, maybe two or three blinks. In a *Business Insider* article about interviewing for a job, Anna Pitts observes, "Everybody knows how important first impressions are. But not everybody knows that the 'first impression' is actually only a seven second window upon first meeting someone. This means in an interview situation you need to act

---

15. Adapted from "Taking Constructive Criticism Like a Champ," Ibid.

quickly in order to make a brilliant first impression on your interviewers."[16]

The "vibes" people pick up in those first moments are their rapid interpretation of how we present ourselves: the expression on our faces, the look in our eyes, our body language, and the first words that we say.

It's a Two-Way Street

As we try to make a good first impression on someone, we're sizing up that person at the same moment.

We often employ one of two losing strategies to change people's minds: intimidation and facts.

It's Very Difficult to Change Someone's Opinion of Us

We often employ one of two losing strategies to change people's minds: intimidation and facts. Some of us insult the other person as "stupid" (or we use more colorful epithets) and others marshal an array of facts to convince the person we're right and they're wrong. One of these is more socially

16. "You Only Have 7 Seconds to Make a First Impression," Anna Pitts, *Business Insider*, April 8, 2013, https://www.businessinsider.com/only-7-seconds-to-make-first-impression-2013-4.

acceptable, but neither one works very well at all. In an article in *Inc.*, Geoffrey James notes, "Facts usually don't change minds because people's beliefs predetermine which facts they consider valid or relevant. The stronger the belief, the more effectively people manage to ignore or discount facts that tend to undermine that belief. When beliefs are strong, contrary facts tend to strengthen rather than weaken those beliefs."[17] This conclusion seems counterintuitive until we realize that a person's preconception of *truth* provides security and confidence, so any challenge causes him to defend the source of his strength. Giving up that source is almost unthinkable.

Our Opinions Shape Others' Opinions

At first glance, this point appears to contradict the previous one, but they are in two different categories. People cling to their cherished opinions if they believe their security is based on it, but if not, they are usually very open to new ideas. For instance, if I tell a friend, "Brenda and I really enjoyed the new Italian restaurant in Buckhead. She had lasagna and I had chicken parmesan. Both were delicious," my friend is unlikely to say, "You're a fool! I don't believe you!" Instead, he'll say, "Thanks for telling me. My wife and I will go there soon." In many cases, our opinions of a

---

17. "How to Change People's Minds," Geoffrey James, *Inc.*, September 7, 2017, https://www.inc.com/geoffrey-james/how-to-change-peoples-minds. html.

product, a vacation spot, a restaurant, or anything else will shape the opinions of the people who value our input.

Some People Share Their Opinions Without Being Asked

When I'm standing in line at the airport, total strangers often decide I'm the perfect person for them to unload their opinions...of the airline...or the weather...or the game last night...or the clothes someone nearby is wearing. The topics are endless and so is the one-sided conversation. I'm not sure why these people feel the freedom or the need to tell me their thoughts about these things, but they do. Generally, I smile for a second, but I don't make eye contact. I hope they get the message. Some do; some don't.

Social Media Is the Most Powerful Purveyor of Opinions

Today, people share photos of dinner, selfies, vacations—you name it—as well as their thoughts on every conceivable topic. We can download apps that collect, categorize, and communicate people's opinions on restaurants, hotels, employers, airlines, cities, books, and every product known to man. Online, everyone is an author and publisher; we can say virtually anything we want, harsh or kind, true or false. Some people turn into raving monsters when their fingers touch a keyboard. They're polite and reasonable in person, but vicious when they post. And if those reading their rants can't distinguish between truth and lies, which is often the case, the lies can easily become reposted thousands or even millions of times. One media expert notes:

> "Opinion Shortage" is one headline you'll never come across.... Sharing on social media is like getting a tattoo. The rule to live by: Once something is posted, it can never be deleted. What usually happens, especially with the controversial, is that people take screenshots and reshare. This is how a lot of posts live for a long time.
>
> If we care about other people and our own reputation, nothing beats being mindful. The best person to sensor you is you. Remember in the age of the Internet, everything that goes online is permanent. And, when it comes to regret, you're more likely going to regret what you publish than what you don't. For the sake of others, and yourself, be mindful.[18]

These concepts tell us that to some degree, we're the architects of people's opinions of us. Certainly, we can't completely control the conclusions they draw about us, but we can be thoughtful about the image we present. I'm not suggesting we practice "image management," which is generally understood as the attempt to cover up our flaws and

---

18. "On Sharing Opinions on Social Media," Blessing Mpofu, *Life and Leadership*, December 30, 2016, https://blessing.im/on-sharing-opinions-on-social-media.

do what we can to convince people to approve of us. My recommendation is for us to value a few people's opinions more than any others—and especially accept God's opinion that He loves us, has forgiven us, and has given us the safety of His grace.

The opinions of some people inspire us, but at least a few are dangerous to our emotional and psychological health.

We need to become skilled at filtering people's opinions and placing values on them on a scale from significant to expendable. The opinions of some people inspire us, but at least a few are dangerous to our emotional and psychological health. When we identify the people who genuinely care for us, we let their opinions sink deep into our minds and hearts, and we invite those people to give us confidence, security, and a vision for a bright future.

About forty-five years ago, when I was a student cooking breakfast in the morning and mopping floors in the afternoon, the college president told me, "Sam, you're really smart. Whatever you touch will turn to gold." That wonderful moment is indelibly engraved in my memory. It has given me confidence when I wondered about my future and strength when I felt alone and weak. One statement of contempt can cause enormous harm, and one statement of affirmation brings life, hope, and peace. The challenge for all of us is to filter out the opinions of people who want to hurt us and let in only the opinions of those who care for us.

The opinion others have of us is our brand.

Think About It:

+ Whose opinion of you has supported, inspired, resourced, and challenged you? Describe the impact that person has had on you.

+ What are some ways to filter others' opinions so you accept only the ones that are helpful?

+ What research can you do to determine the opinions that other people—customers, clients, parishioners, employees, etc.—have of your leadership and your organization?

You will find, if you think for a moment, that the people who influence you are the people who believe in you.   —Henry Drummond, British banker, writer, and member of Parliament

4

YOUR OPINION MATTERS
Our conclusions have incredible power to change lives.

Leaders hire me for my opinions. It still amazes me that I never pastored a church larger than a hundred and fifty people, but I consult with pastors who have churches of more than 10,000—and they look to me for fresh ideas. One of the waves of innovation in the church today is multisite. Many churches are opening satellite campuses to reach people, make it convenient for those who live far from the main campus, and expand the church's influence.

Pastors feel more than a little angst about using videos from the previous week that were shot at the mother church, or a live stream, or a live person at each site who's not the lead pastor. They often feel that if they make the wrong decision, their strategy will collapse. I try to give them some peace of mind when I tell them, "Why don't you try all three and see how they work for you?" Instantly, I can see the look on their faces change from worry to excitement.

As I consult with leaders of all kinds of organizations, almost without exception, they want to talk about one of their staff members who isn't doing a good job. Some of these leaders have tried for years to make a square peg fit into a round hole, and they've finally given up. Now they've concluded they need to fire the person. As we talk, I explain that every leader has three main options for each employee, manager, or staff member. They can *retain* them in the same position and provide more training and resources; they can conclude the person has value, but doesn't fit in the current role and needs to be *reassigned*; or they may realize the person doesn't fit the organization's culture, no matter what position they may be assigned, and the person needs to be *released*. Quite often, this simple set of options helps the leader observe the situation more clearly, resolves the leader's opinion of the person, and provides clarity about the best opportunity for the person and the organization, even if that means releasing him.

EARNING RESPECT

I've talked with leaders who complained that their people are resistant to their ideas and perhaps even defiant.

They tell me, "I don't know what's wrong. No matter what I say, they find reasons why it won't work." As I spend time with the leader and the team, I sometimes realize the leader has created a "yes, but" culture.

Leaders who find their people resist or defy their ideas may have inadvertently created a "yes, but" culture.

When people on the team have proposed ideas, the leader has shot them down so many times that the team is returning fire! The problem is on both sides, but the solution starts with the leader. I explain the importance of a different response: "Yes and..." The leader doesn't have to buy every idea that members of the team generate, but every idea needs to be valued. Instead of rolling his eyes, sighing, and moving on to his own idea, the leader needs to say, "That's an interesting idea. Tell me more about it." After listening, the leader might say, "I see what you're getting at. What if we did it this way...?" This approach takes more time, but it leaves people feeling heard, understood, and valued. It *gives* respect and therefore *earns* respect.

My rule of thumb is that respect, like love, covers a multitude of organizational sins. It doesn't make those problems vanish into thin air, but it takes the sting out of disagreements. Without a baseline of respect, every disagreement can be interpreted as a fight for survival. But with respect, people feel secure enough to disagree without labeling the other person as a fool.

For my team, I look for "yes and" people, but to keep them positive and creative, they need to see me as a "yes and" leader. I appreciate people who have new ideas and push me to think more broadly to find better solutions, but only if we enjoy mutual respect. If I sense the person is demanding her way instead of offering it, I realize I have a bigger problem than finding a solution to the problem we're discussing. The benchmarks for me are whether a person will give full voice to creative ideas and then, after the decision is made, dive in to make it happen, even if the final decision wasn't what she recommended.

All of us can get so wrapped up in our agenda that we lose sight of the bigger picture and the roles of the people around us. I recommend that all of us regularly go back to the first question in this book:

How did I get here: in this place, at this time, and in this role?

When we recognize that we're the product of others' observations, opinions, and the opportunities they gave us, we'll be more mindful of the importance of providing those treasures for the people on our teams.

RIGHT ASSESSMENTS

Our opinions of others need to be accurate, not skewed by our personal preferences. For instance, creative people are seldom good planners and those who are detailed administrators generally aren't very innovative. If I'm on the creative end of the spectrum, do I value the people who work through all the details to keep a project on track, or do I dismiss them as second-class? Or if I'm an engineer who lives by spreadsheets, do I assume creative people are nuts because they don't think like me?

One of the most common mistakes leaders make is selecting the wrong person to be in charge of a project. Quite often, they pick the one who has talked a lot in the staff meeting. This person is excited, shares points from an article, and gives plenty of ideas about how the suggestion can be successful. A lot of verbalization, though, doesn't always translate into organizational skills. The person who should be assigned responsibility may not have said a word. I know this is true because I've seen it many times. In meetings, Brenda is usually silent as she takes copious notes. Other people eagerly contribute to the conversation about solving a problem or moving a project forward, and she takes it all in without saying a word. I know from experience that she is the best administrator on the team. If I want something done on time and done right, I'll give her the responsibility.

Far too often, leaders discount the quiet people on the team. I've heard them complain, "That person just sits there. He's not engaged at all. I don't even know why he's on our team." That may be an accurate assessment, but more often than not, the person is like Brenda, silent in meetings but gifted in making things happen behind the scenes. We need to look beyond our initial observations to see what's really there and then form an opinion based on the facts.

*We have rapport with people who are just like us...
and we're a bit suspicious of those who bring
something different to the table.*

Why do we often make the wrong assumption about quiet people? Because *like likes like*—we have rapport with people who are just like us. We value them. And we're a bit suspicious of those who bring something different to the table. Leaders are talkers, so they naturally notice others who verbalize clearly and often. Since they achieved success with their speaking ability, they assume that people who are quiet have very little to offer.

I could give a host of illustrations, but let me share just one. Larry was on a leadership team at his software company.

At every meeting, he had great ideas and he expressed them with clarity and emotion. When he spoke to the team he led, he powerfully motivated them. Larry was such a gifted speaker that department managers in the company asked him to speak to their teams. Before long, he was a legend in the company. The CEO was so impressed that he made Larry a vice president.

However, within weeks, responsibilities assigned to Larry were lagging behind. He missed deadlines, but he always had excuses. As months passed, Larry spent more of his time speaking—to anyone who would listen—but the people on his team were about to scream because he didn't give them direction. The CEO tried to help by giving Larry an additional administrator and cutting back on his responsibilities, but the CEO finally concluded that Larry was, in fact, the worst administrator he had ever known. The CEO (and everyone else in the company) had been wowed by Larry's talent for speaking, but they formed the wrong opinion that he could translate his skills in articulation into actual productivity.

Have you ever assigned an important responsibility to someone who is a good talker, but had trouble completing the task? Have you assumed that someone who is quiet is disengaged and disinterested? I'm certainly not suggesting that all quiet people are brilliant administrators, but I'm recommending that leaders become savvy about their people.

Like likes like, so be aware that your opinion of people is almost certainly colored by your own strengths. When our opinions are based on inaccurate observations, we ask thinking people to do, doing people to think, innovative people to organize, and organized people to be innovative—and these errors frustrate everyone.

THE HIERARCHY OF INFLUENCE

When we think about shaping the opinions of the people in an organization, it's helpful to realize that some have more influence than others. This isn't a value statement about any individual; it's merely an observation about the way things work.

In most organizations, one person has the role of originator, like Steve Jobs at Apple. Several people take this person's creative ideas and shape them into a workable, practical plan. Many people are then involved in creating the products or leading the activities. And finally, the people who benefit tell others about what they've experienced and invite them to buy or join.

As a leader, I don't expect everyone in an organization to be creative and I'm not surprised when only a few can do the detailed planning. The vision for the impact of the product, service, or program should be exciting for everyone involved in every level of the organization. And then, as the public sees the value, they become *evangelists* to tell everyone they know how their lives have been changed.

CHANGING OUR MINDS

We don't like to change our minds. In fact, we avoid it like the plague! Even when we're confronted with undeniable facts that refute our opinions, we find ways to justify what we already believe. In a *Wall Street Journal* article, Steven Sloman observes:

> We are not great reasoners. Most people don't like to think at all, or like to think as little as possible. And by most, I mean roughly 70 percent of the population. Even the rest seem to devote a lot of their resources to justifying beliefs that they want to hold, as opposed to forming credible beliefs based only on fact.[19]

To overcome our fierce resistance to changing our opinions about people, ideas, or events, we need to understand their hold on us. We can identify at least three main ways people form opinions: first, having a past that has affected them deeply. For instance, an adult who was emotionally abused by an alcoholic parent almost inevitably feels worthless and believes their opinions matter little to those in

19. "Forming Opinions," Steven Sloman, *Wall Street Journal*, March 15, 2019, https://www.wsj.com/articles/notable-quotable-forming-opinions-1492365942.

authority. It takes a lot of new, positive, and respectful experiences to chip away at the Gibraltar of this ingrained (and, at least on one level, thoroughly reasonable) fear. Second, studious, reflective people form their opinions based on the preponderance of evidence. They conduct meticulous research and consider the validity of the sources they examine. After they've come to a conclusion, they're very reluctant to value the opinion of someone who hasn't done similarly exhaustive research to back their beliefs. And third, still others are like the elders of the Areopagus (see Acts 17:19–21), who delighted in hearing all sides of an argument. Their conclusions are based on the relative strength of each person's stated and defended position.

We're wise to stretch our mental faculties,
to work hard to see things from a different angle,
if only to understand those who disagree with us.

We're wise to stretch our mental faculties, to work hard to see things from a different angle, if only to understand those who disagree with us. Irish author St. John Ervine recommended drastic action: "Every man…should periodically be compelled to listen to opinions which are infuriating to him. To hear nothing but what is pleasing to one is to make a pillow of the mind."[20]

Our natural defensiveness is based on the stark assumption that "being wrong is a kind of death." Psychologist Greg Lester says our beliefs are so strong because we associate them with survival:

> Even beliefs that do not seem clearly or directly connected to survival…are still closely connected to survival. This is because beliefs do not occur individually or in a vacuum. They are related to one another in a tightly interlocking system that creates the brain's fundamental view of the nature of the world. It is this system that the brain relies on in order to experience consistency, control, cohesion, and safety in the world. It must maintain this system intact in order to feel that survival is being successfully accomplished.
>
> This means that even seemingly small, inconsequential beliefs can be as integral to the brain's experience of survival as are beliefs that are "obviously" connected to survival. Thus, trying to change *any* belief, no matter how small or silly it may seem, can produce ripple effects through the entire system and ultimately threaten the brain's experience of

20. Sewell Stokes, *Pilloried!* (New York: D. Appleton & Co., 1929).

survival. This is why people are so often driven to defend even seemingly small or tangential beliefs.[21]

This clarifies why it's so hard to change our opinions, but it doesn't excuse our bull-headedness. We certainly don't need to question every belief all the time, but when we're confronted with a new set of facts, when we have no other choice, or when the laws of the state require compliance, we need to find the courage to see things from a different angle. For instance, we may have assumed that we couldn't make it on our own, but the death of our spouse forces us to find a way. We may have believed that our current job is the perfect one, but downsizing layoffs cause us to find other employment. We may assume that driving fifteen miles an hour over the speed limit is perfectly acceptable until we see the flashing lights behind us.

We often have more options than we realize. We may feel stuck in a job with a demanding boss, but if we don't see opportunities for another job near where we live, we may not think we can leave. However, this poses several paths we might choose. We can look for a better position in another city and live with the changes a geographical move will cause for our family; we can look for a job in our community; we can try to resolve things with the boss so we can enjoy our work; or we can develop a thicker skin and not take every

21. "Why Bad Beliefs Don't Die," Gregory W. Lester, *Skeptical Inquirer*, November/December 2000, https://skepticalinquirer.org/2000/11/why_bad_beliefs_dont_die.

comment personally. Our opinion of the boss and the situation can lead to a dead end in our thinking, or it can lead to us considering a range of options. We can be the recipients of what might be called *vicarious wisdom*.

For example, Mark and his younger brother Brad were talking one day. Mark commented, "You know, I'm impressed that you've made a lot of really good decisions with your life."

Brad smiled. "I watched you and did the opposite."

Mark laughed. "Smart. Really smart."

We can gain the wisdom of accurate opinions in a number of different ways. The best is to understand the principles of wisdom and conform our lives around them. Next is watching the people near us, noting how their choices played out, copying the good ones and rejecting the ones that led to problems. And last, we suffer the consequences of so many unwise decisions that we finally have to learn.

PAUL HAD TO LEARN, TOO

The apostle Paul was one of the most brilliant thinkers and one of the most effective leaders in history. Today, two millennia after he lived, we still study his writings. And today, about a third of the people on earth follow the teachings about Jesus that Paul formalized.[22] He was a passionate, driven man who didn't stop when he encountered severe beatings, ridicule, and other threats to his life. But like many people who are like this, he could be prickly.

After Paul met Christ on the road to Damascus, his life turned around. He had been attacking the followers of Jesus and, suddenly, he started proclaiming Jesus as God's Messiah. Paul first spoke in Damascus, but the Jews there plotted to assassinate him. He escaped over a wall and fled to Jerusalem. Paul expected to be warmly received by the disciples as a new convert to the faith, but they were suspicious that his "Damascus road experience" was only a ruse. They believed Paul was trying to infiltrate the church so he could capture its leaders. At that critical moment when he was alone, one man stood up for Paul: Barnabas, "the son of encouragement," who had been a generous and faithful leader since the first days after Pentecost. With Barnabas defending Paul and vouching for the authenticity of his faith, the disciples accepted him. Not surprisingly, the two men became fast friends.

Sometime later, when Paul and Barnabas were in Antioch, the church leaders fasted and prayed and they

---

22. "Christians remain world's largest religious group, but they are declining in Europe," Conrad Hackett and David McClendon, Pew Research Center, April 5, 2017, https://www.pewresearch.org/fact-tank/2017/04/05/christians-remain-worlds-largest-religious-group-but-they-are-declining-in-europe.

were led to send the two men on a missionary journey to cities in the middle of what is now Turkey. They took Barnabas's cousin, John Mark, with them. On their first stop on the island of Cyprus, they shared the gospel with Sergius Paulus, the leading official, but Elymas, a magician, tried to turn the official away from the faith. After a while, Paul had had enough. He turned to Elymas and said, *"You are a child of the devil and an enemy of everything that is right! You are full of all kinds of deceit and trickery. Will you never stop perverting the right ways of the Lord? Now the hand of the Lord is against you. You are going to be blind for a time, not even able to see the light of the sun"* (Acts 13:10–11). Elymas was instantly blinded and helpless. Sergius Paulus was then convinced that Jesus was the Messiah, just as Paul and Barnabas proclaimed.

The historian, Luke, doesn't give us any details, but he tells us that before their next stop, John Mark left the group and went back to Jerusalem. Paul and Barnabas continued their journey, traveling to Cyprus, Pisidian Antioch, Iconium, Lystra, and Derbe. In every city, they spoke about Christ and encountered severe opposition. In Lystra, God used Paul to heal a crippled man and the people there concluded the two men were the Greek gods Zeus and Hermes. They tried to offer a bull as a sacrifice to them, but Paul and Barnabas tore their garments as Paul pleaded with them to stop. In the next scene, hostile Jews from Pisidian Antioch showed up and convinced the people of Lystra that Paul and

Barnabas were charlatans. They stoned Paul, dragged him out of the city, and left him for dead. If he did actually die, God resuscitated him and he kept going on the journey.

When they got back to Antioch, Paul and Barnabas had incredible stories about the power of God working in the lives of both Jews and Gentiles. However, some of the leading Jewish Christians in Jerusalem were concerned that this new faith was breaking too many boundaries. They believed the Gentiles first needed to become Jewish before they could follow Jesus. In one of the most consequential meetings in church history, the Jerusalem Council met to hear both sides. Finally, James decreed that Gentiles who believed were considered full members of the church without becoming Jewish.

After the council, Paul asked Barnabas to go with him to visit the churches they had planted. Barnabas wanted to take John Mark along, but Paul didn't trust the young man who had abandoned them even before they encountered such hostility in the cities of central Turkey. He flatly refused to let John Mark go with them. Luke tells us, *"They had such a sharp disagreement that they parted company. Barnabas took Mark and sailed for Cyprus, but Paul chose Silas and left, commended by the believers to the grace of the Lord. He went through Syria and Cilicia, strengthening the churches"* (Acts 15:39–41).

I wanted to give the background of this disagreement because we need to understand that Paul was willing to discard Barnabas, the man who had stood up for him when no one else believed him, the man who had been his trusted partner in his first great evangelistic enterprise, the one who had shared the blessings and hardships of serving Jesus. Barnabas had patience and grace for his cousin, a young man who had failed. He believed in giving him a second chance. Paul didn't. The two men separated and we don't hear about Barnabas again.

That, however, isn't the end of the story. Years later, after more grueling journeys to take the gospel to the far reaches of the empire, Paul was arrested twice. During his second arrest, shortly before he was to be beheaded, Paul wrote his last letter. In the stinking dungeon in Rome, Paul's letter to Timothy is both courageous and desperate. Near the end, he has some personal requests: *"Do your best to come to me quickly, for Demas, because he loved this world, has deserted me and has gone to Thessalonica. Crescens has gone to Galatia, and Titus to Dalmatia. Only Luke is with me. Get Mark and bring him with you, because he is helpful to me in my ministry"* (2 Timothy 4:9–11). From this short passage, we get a sense that Paul greatly values loyalty—to Jesus, to the mission, and to Paul himself. Some, like Demas, have bolted and left the mission (like John Mark had done years before), but we see a surprising request: find Mark, bring him to me *"because he is helpful to me in my ministry."* This, I believe, says far more about the change in Paul's opinion of John Mark than it does about John Mark's opinion of Paul.

I can imagine this change in Paul didn't happen quickly, but it happened. Similarly, our opinions of others may not change easily, but change *is* possible.

THE POWER OF OPINIONS

Our view of a person, and our verbalization of that view, has incredible power to shape the lives of the people around us. As business leaders, pastors, parents, or friends, we play an important role in their future. Our opinions have the ability to:

- *Promote*: move people higher, affirm their talents, and confirm their direction

- *Demote*: move them down to a different role where they can thrive

- *Stagnate*: give them confidence to stay where they are because they're in the role that fits them best

- *Terminate*: when attempts to find the right fit and provide enough resources have failed, it's time to release them

Don't take your impact on others for granted. You may not have a lofty position or an impressive title, but all of us make a difference. Study your thinking patterns, analyze your observations, and form an opinion of the accuracy of your opinions. When you understand the power of your opinions, you'll use them like a surgeon's scalpel to heal, like a coach's confidence to inspire, and like a captain's map to guide.

Don't take your impact on others for granted.
You may not have a lofty position or an impressive title,
but all of us make a difference.

In Part One, we looked at the importance of fine-tuning our skills of observation. In this section, we explored the power of opinions. Next, we'll examine the ways we can open doors of opportunity for people.

Think About It:

+ How do you respond to "yes, but" people? Are you one of them? Explain your answer.

+ How does the principle of "like likes like" show up in your relationships?

+ What are some specific ways the power of your opinions can be more positive?

If your actions inspire others to dream more, learn more, do more and become more, you are a leader.

— John Quincy Adams,
sixth president of the United States

PART THREE
OPPORTUNITIES

5

THE PEOPLE STANDING AT OUR DOORS
They've given us opportunities.

Several years ago, I stood in front of the leaders of <u>Inspire Church in Honolulu, Hawaii,</u> led by Pastors Mike and Lisa Kai. The church was planted in 2001 and has since grown to four campuses, with thousands in attendance. It was an honor to be asked to speak there. How did it happen? How did I have this opportunity?

I had been a pastor, too, but it was a small country church. Our largest attendance on a Sunday was about a hundred and fifty people—and that only happened because we served free food that day. Most of the time, about a hundred people showed up. My pastoral experience certainly didn't give me a platform to speak in one of the largest and finest churches in the world!

Months before I spoke at Inspire Church, a casual conversation took place. Pastor Benny Perez, who is the lead pastor of Church LV in Las Vegas, Nevada, a multi-site church serving thousands of people, was riding in a car with Pastor Mike from the Honolulu airport to Inspire Church. I had consulted with Pastor Benny and it seems my input was valuable enough for him to ask Pastor Mike, "Do you know Sam Chand?"

Pastor Mike didn't know me at the time, so he shook his head. Pastor Benny told him how he had learned about me, contacted me, and invited me to consult with him. He then explained how my input had been beneficial.

At that moment, Pastor Mike formed an opinion of me based on the affirmation of Pastor Benny. Pastor Mike called me and asked me to fly to Hawaii to consult with him. My opportunity to have an impact at his church—on him in his role as the pastor, with his staff, and with all of the leaders at his church—came because Pastor Benny shared his observations and opinions about me and the trust in their relationship gave Pastor Mike the confidence to call me to ask for my help.

That's how at least 90 percent of my opportunities happen. It's all about establishing relationships based on trust and respect, and people who benefit telling their friends. Many of them call me and ask me to help them in the same way I've helped the person who recommended me.

OPPORTUNITIES ARE NOT GUARANTEES

Every opportunity is the product of observations and opinions that opened doors of possibilities. Opportunities, though, are just that; they aren't guarantees. Sometimes, things work far better than we could have dreamed, but occasionally, they bomb. It's my responsibility to cultivate the opportunity and make the best of it. For me, that means I listen far more than I talk. Over the years, I've learned to ask plenty of questions so I can have a lot of data points. Each of them is an observation and, together, they help me form opinions about what the leader really needs—which, more often than not, is different from what was expressed over the phone in the initial conversation.

Sometimes, things work far better than we could have dreamed, but occasionally, they bomb.

The news is full of sordid reports of church and business leaders who have squandered their opportunities. High-profile leaders and under-the-radar ones have been identified in incidents of adultery and sexual abuse, even of minors and staff members. Financial mismanagement is another way leaders are forfeiting their opportunity to have a positive impact on their communities. And some leaders have been released because they came to the conclusion they were emperors rather than shepherds.

All of these people were *observed*, although they tried to keep their behavior secret as long as possible and almost always denied it when someone called them out. People formed new *opinions* of them, usually very begrudgingly because they couldn't believe the accusations at first. And finally, the wonderful *opportunity* they had enjoyed was theirs no more.

Is it possible for these leaders to reclaim a good opinion? Certainly—but it's not easy. The road back is often long and difficult; many don't have the courage to take it. These leaders didn't lose their intelligence, their organizational skills, or their ability to communicate, but they did lose their opportunity to lead because someone observed a flaw that they had tried to hide.

All of us need to find someone to confide in before we go too far down the wrong road. If not, we learn to live with secrets and before long, our lies take on a life of their own. We need to be brutally honest about our deepest fears and our attempts to manage our image to keep people from seeing us sweat.

COMMON FEARS AMONG LEADERS

Some of the most common fears in the lives of leaders include:

Fear of Criticism

We want to be seen as successful, competent, and wise. We may want to project toughness, but many of us have very thin skins and are deeply wounded by criticism.

The solution isn't to bark back at those who have something negative to say about us. A better strategy is to embrace the fear and regularly ask for feedback from our teams and trusted friends who aren't part of the organization, including coaches and consultants. We'll learn a lot, we'll disarm those who say we can't take it, and we'll create a more open, vibrant environment.

Fear of Being Wrong

It's one thing to be privately criticized—we can often deflect it, blame others, or deny it happened—but it's something else entirely when our error is revealed in plain sight. Many of us thrive on always being right, always having the answer, and always being respected as the smartest person in the room.

We have two options when we make a mistake: we can see being wrong as a catastrophe, or we can see it as a normal part of growing and learning. The first produces fierce defensiveness; the other breaks down walls and invites people to be part of the solution.

Fear of Not Measuring Up

We'd never tell anyone, maybe not even our spouse, but from time to time, many of us consider other career options. This may be a normal and temporary desire to escape the strain of leading people, but it can become an obsession. We can spend endless hours daydreaming about getting out of our current roles and finding something more meaningful... or at least easier.

Fear of Being Exposed as a Fraud

Many leaders believe the only way to set the pace for their organizations is to be relentlessly positive, even when they feel deeply discouraged. This dual life is self-perpetuating because people would be aghast if these leaders took off their masks for even a brief moment and confessed their worries and doubts. These leaders simply can't envision letting that happen to them.

Fear of Running on Empty

Leaders can give, serve, and sacrifice until they have nothing left in the tank. They work hard to keep their teams and everyone in the organization highly motivated, but they may feel utterly empty.

Fear of Making Hard Decisions

The burden of leadership weighs heavy, especially when things aren't working out the way we planned. We'd like to dodge the strain and find a nice, quiet beach in the Caribbean, but we have to keep plodding ahead, facing each decision with as much courage as we can muster.

In an article in *Forbes*, Brent Gleeson, a former Navy SEAL, combat veteran, and an entrepreneur, encourages leaders to focus on their team as a resource instead of letting their fears overwhelm them:

> As the saying goes, with much power comes much responsibility. You are not just responsible to clients and shareholders. Your first priority is to your team. If you put them first, all the rest will fall into place. Being responsible for a person's livelihood can be a stressful burden. As a leader your role is to define the mission, provide resources, and remove obstacles. Embrace the fact that you have a team to lead. It's a good problem to have. Assuming you have the right people doing the right things, remember that they can be your best resource for important information. Keep them in the loop and ask them to do the same for you. Working together as a team will lighten that burden of responsibility.[23]

23. "Conquering the Common Fears of Leadership," Brent Gleeson, Forbes, May 5, 2014, https://www.forbes.com/sites/brentgleeson/2014/05/05/conquering-the-common-fears-of-leadership/#6d0d2e6c673c.

WHAT LEADERS NEED

To handle the fears and strains of leadership, we need a friend, a coach, or a consultant who will speak the truth to us—the hard truth as well as the encouraging truth. And we need to be appropriately vulnerable with the people we lead.

To handle the fears and strains of leadership, we need a friend, a coach, or a consultant who will speak the truth to us— the hard truth as well as the encouraging truth.

Of course, this doesn't mean that we *air it all out* with everyone all the time. That would be foolish. But we need to give at least one person permission to ask us absolutely any question and we need to answer it honestly. We don't need a hundred safe people, but we absolutely must have at least one—and preferably several.

The need for authenticity isn't limited to organizational leaders. In every significant relationship—marriage, parenting, with co-workers, and with friends—people are observing us, forming opinions of us, and either promoting us to new opportunities or demoting us by avoiding us, or gossiping about us, or we stagnate in a dead-end relationship without joy and creativity, and sometimes, the connection is severed and the relationship is terminated.

IT'S NOT ROCKET SCIENCE

Everybody wants bigger and better opportunities: a better job, more money, greater purpose, more robust health, and a happier family. Over the years, I've talked to plenty of people who complained that they haven't been given enough (or big enough) opportunities. They often point to factors they believe have held them back, such as a lack of education, financial limitations, family background, ethnicity and prejudice, and a less-than-stellar reputation based on the review of a past boss. I don't doubt that these things are hurdles, but they don't need to be impenetrable barriers that eliminate opportunities.

Actually, the only true barrier is the mind-set that says, "My condition is unfair, permanent, and crippling." It may, in fact, be unfair, but it doesn't have to be permanent or crippling. With courage, creativity, and tenacity, we can still walk through the doors of opportunity.

How? Opportunities come when people observe that we're trustworthy and competent, they form an opinion that they can trust us, and only then will they open a door for us. Many people expect the door to open without them doing the hard work of changing people's observations and opinions.

This connection isn't hard to grasp. If I want to buy a new car, but my credit score is low, the bank will make this observation and form an opinion that they can't trust me with the money I need to buy the car. I can blame the loan officer all I want to, but fury doesn't change the situation. The solution is for me to work hard to pay bills on time and save enough money for a down payment. I can also take out smaller loans and create a history of paying them back on time. Gradually, my credit score will rise and when it's high enough, I can go back to the bank. This time, the bank employee will observe my financial status, form a new opinion that I'm worthy of a loan, and give me the opportunity to buy the car.

Many people expect the door of opportunity to open without them doing the hard work of changing people's observations and opinions.

Let me take our responsibility a step farther. If I want to start a business and I need to borrow a lot of money, I'll go to several banks three years before I plan to launch the company and tell them my plans. The loan officers can explain what they require and what they provide. Each year before

I need the money, I go back to have another talk with the three loan officers. In each visit, I bring an audit of my business plan and projected balance sheet, so everything is very clear to me and the loan officers. I'm doing due diligence and I'm inviting the bank to do due diligence well ahead of the time I need the loan. By the time I'm ready to ask for a loan, I know that I've met their requirements and I can choose which bank looks most favorable. From the beginning of this three-year process, the inherent question I've asked is: what does the loan officer need to observe in order to give me a loan when I need it?

If I wait until the month before the business launch to go to the bank, I won't have a strong relationship with a loan officer; I would only guess at the bank's requirements and I probably won't get a loan. I can claim that the loan officer is being unfair, but it will be my fault that I didn't cultivate the relationship in which he could observe me over time and form a positive opinion of my willingness to jump through the bank's hoops. That's the reason I didn't get the loan.

We're only stuck if we believe we're stuck. If we're convinced we have it in our power to change the minds of others, the door of opportunity will eventually open. We need to remember that the camera is always on and it's always on us. What do people see? If they see us complaining and blaming others for our plight, they have every reason to wonder if they can trust us. But all great stories are about heroes who overcome long odds. Difficulties are fertile soil for a hero to display courage and determination. The question people are asking about us is always: is this person a courageous hero, or is he a victim who blames others for his problems? They're watching. What do they see?

Observations lead to opinions lead to opportunities— or not. The only piece of the equation we can control is the observations people make of us. We can present ourselves as diligent, honorable people, but we can't control the opinions they draw from their observations and we certainly can't control their willingness to open doors for us. This means our focus has to be on crafting what they observe. If their observations are less than positive, their opinions will be shaded and they won't give us opportunities. But if they see admirable traits, they'll form the opinion that we're trustworthy and they'll give us chances to prove ourselves.

The only piece of the equation we can control is the observations people make of us.

I had to work hard to cultivate positive observations with Brenda's parents when we were dating. They had never had a meaningful relationship with another foreigner. I didn't exactly bring a sterling background to the table. I wasn't a citizen of the United States and I didn't have very good prospects for a job. I didn't have a house; I didn't even have an apartment. Her parents were more than a little apprehensive about entrusting me with their beloved daughter!

I only had two things going for me: I had a car and a church in Oregon had offered me a job as their youth pastor. The pastor told me, "We can't pay you, but we'll provide you with an apartment." That was a move up for me!

I knew I had a long way to go to convince Brenda's parents to give us their blessing. When I discovered that her father was going to put new siding on their house, I showed up to help. It didn't matter how hard it was, he wasn't going to hear a word of complaint from me. We worked long hours for two weeks to install that siding. I think it was the very best way for me to connect with him and begin to prove myself.

Before and after Brenda and I were married, I never asked her parents for money. Gradually, they concluded that I was a hardworking, respectful, and trustworthy young man who genuinely loved their daughter. They had no hopes that I'd make it big and be able to buy Brenda the finest things, but they believed I'd make enough for us to live on.

MAKING A GREAT FIRST IMPRESSION

Whether you're meeting your prospective in-laws, a new friend, a neighbor, or someone from human resources, it's important to make a great first impression. Here are four *be's* to remember:

Be Yourself

Don't try to impress the person. Instead, make it your goal to have a meaningful first connection. This distinction matters! If you try to impress someone, you'll probably come across as phony, a poser. People can tell if you're faking it and they appreciate meeting someone who is genuine.

Be Relaxed

The first thing people notice, even before you say a word, is your body language. It shouts your underlying message, especially if it's very different from your words. For instance, if you say, "It's nice to meet you," but you're tense, roll your eyes, or don't make eye contact, you're communicating, "It's really *not* that nice to meet you!"

For an important occasion, such as a job interview or a sales meeting with a prospective buyer, watch your tone of voice and volume. If you come on too strong, you'll be perceived as pushy. If you're too meek, you'll be perceived as less than confident in both yourself and your message.

It's a good idea to practice in front of a mirror. Stand up, move toward the mirror like you're meeting someone, hold out your hand and say, "Hello, I'm Sam," or whatever your name is—don't tell people you're me! "It's good to meet you." Did you smile? Did you slouch? Did you look relaxed? Would *you* want to meet you?

Be Interested in the Other Person

We make the best impressions when we take the focus off ourselves and show genuine interest in the other person. A simple, "Tell me about yourself" is a great way to get the conversation going. Ask more questions than you answer and ask follow-up questions to find out more. Everyone wants to be perceived as knowledgeable and we're most knowledgeable about our own lives. When we make the other person the center of attention, we're saying, "You're important to me."

Why do we talk too much when we meet people? There may be several reasons, including the fact that we want to impress them with what we know, we feel insecure and filling up the space with our words prevents awkward pauses, and we may be, after all, self-absorbed and don't care very much about others.

If you're in a job interview, it's not appropriate to ask the HR person about their life, but it's entirely appropriate to ask about the company's culture, history, goals, and values.

These questions show that you understand the importance of what they bring to the table and it's not all about you.

Be Gracious

You can certainly share your opinions, but avoid being demanding or dogmatic. Today, people have very polarized conceptions of politics and this spills out into extreme views about virtually everything. It's perfectly fine to disagree, but not to draw your sword, or worse, draw blood! You can wait until another day to talk about your disagreements. The first conversation should open doors, not close them. When people walk away from you, you want them to think, *I really like that person and I want to talk more.*

It's important to build bridges between the two of you. In an article in *Inc.*, Dan Veltri, cofounder and chief product officer of Weebly, says:

> I've found that the key to a lasting first impression is to discuss a topic that both you and the person care about, ask insightful questions to better understand their point of view, and then provide a new perspective on their thinking based on your own experiences. This not only shows the person that you're listening but also provides them with lasting value. At some point, if you need something from

that person, not only will they remember you, but they will be happy to help.[24]

OPPORTUNITIES HELP US ACHIEVE OUR GOALS

When we have a goal, we look for opportunities to reach it. We can certainly have individual goals that don't rely on others, but the vast majority of what makes life meaningful is worked out in relationships. Thus, making a good impression on people is essential.

+ If a person wants the opportunity to work at a company, what does she want the HR officer to observe about her?

+ If a pastor or church leader wants visitors to have the opportunity to become participants and members, what do newcomers need to observe about the church and its people?

+ If a young man wants the opportunity to take a young lady out for a date, what does she need to observe about him?

+ If a company wants the opportunity to expand its customer base and sell more products, what do the prospective customers need to observe about the products?

---

24. "12 Tips on How to Make a Great First Impression, According to Executives," Christina DesMarais, *Inc.*, February 19, 2017, https://www.inc.com/christina-desmarais/12-tips-on-how-to-make-a-great-first-impression-according-to-executives.html.

+ If a young person wants the opportunity to play on a sports team, what skills and attitude does the coach need to observe?

We could make an endless list of connections between observations leading to opinions and then to opportunities. All advertising is designed to craft observations that result in good opinions and buying opportunities. All of our interactions with people are filled with possibilities to present ourselves so they observe something good, noble, and desirable, and then take the opportunity to get to know us better.

NOTHING WE CAN DO...

Don't be surprised when some people aren't as excited about your opportunities as you are. My time as the president of the college was very fulfilling. We had seen the student population grow by almost 1,000 percent, we had achieved accreditation, and the college was on firm financial footing. I had hired some very fine people to serve as vice presidents and gave them important responsibilities and they made my life easier. Personally, I thoroughly enjoyed the role and I was making a level of income I had only dreamed about a few years earlier, when I cooked breakfasts and swabbed floors. In many ways, the poor, inarticulate young man from India had *arrived*.

Then, in 2003, I resigned.

Even as the college prospered while I was president, a sense of godly discontent grew in me. I felt there was something else I could do with my life...something different... something more. When I announced that I was going to resign, many people thought I had lost my mind! I'm sure some of them wondered if I was having a mid-life crisis.

They had every reason to wonder. By this time in my career as a college president, I had earned the respect of our faculty and I was asked to speak at a wide range of events. I served as an unofficial adviser to leaders of many organizations. If I quit my position as college president, I would leave a respected position, the safety of a network of people I trusted and who trusted me, and the security of a regular paycheck.

At first, I stepped into a part-time role as an outside consultant—and I enjoyed it so much that I realized this was what I was *made* to do. However, to do it with everything in me, I'd have to leave the safety of my role at the college and step into the unknown of becoming a full-time consultant, with no existing clients and no safety net. That's why people thought I was nuts.

As I look back, I realize it was one of the best decisions of my life.

HANDS ON THE HANDLE

I've had, and continue to have, opportunities that boggle my mind. When I was a poor college student, the administrators gave me the opportunity to earn my keep by working before and after my classes. Brenda's parents took perhaps the biggest risk of letting their daughter marry a man from India with very few prospects. Then, a few brave pastors asked me to preach weeklong revivals. Often, there were less than a dozen people in the congregations, but these were wonderful experiences. The pastors fed me, gave me a bed to sleep in, and, at the end of the week, paid me $100 or less, which was barely enough money to pay for the gas to get to the next revival. Whenever a pastor called and asked if I could preach at their church for a whole week, I instantly said, "Yes!" I didn't have to check my calendar. When people told me, "I'm glad you're here, Sam," I wanted to respond, "Hey, I'm glad to be anywhere!"

A little church in Michigan opened their doors to invite me to be their pastor and a college tapped me as their president. John Maxwell believed in me and he came to see me because two men recommended me to him. I appreciate those who have asked me to speak at their events, even with my Indian accent.

Over and over again, people have taken risks to give me opportunities. Church and business leaders have opened their doors to invite me to speak into their lives and help them shape the future of their organizations. My publishers have believed that my manuscripts were worth their investments. I've been asked to serve on a number of boards and consult with the leaders of several denominations. Today, people ask me to tell them my fees, they fly me business class, and they put me up in the finest hotels so I'll be comfortable before and after I speak to their groups. But these incredible moments happen only because literally hundreds of people observed something positive about me, formed a good opinion, and gave me opportunities to speak, teach, consult, and serve.

These examples are just a few of the people who have stood at my door of opportunity and were willing to open it for me. I'll always be grateful to them.

Think About It:

+ Why is it important to realize the only part of the equation we can control is what others observe about us?

+ Do you agree or disagree with this statement: "Everybody wants opportunities." Explain your answer.

+ Do a quick mental scan of your life. Who are the people who have taken a risk to give you an opportunity?

I usually make up my mind about a man in ten seconds, and I very rarely change it.

—Margaret Thatcher,
former Prime Minister of Great Britain

6

OUR HANDS ON THEIR DOORS
*Providing opportunities for the
people around you.*

I've already told the story about how the college gave me a couple of jobs when I didn't have a work permit. And I've explained that the college president spoke words of vision and hope into my life when he said he believed I would succeed at anything I tried to do. These doors were opened when I had very little to offer anyone. Years later, *I* became the president. When I sensed it was time to leave, we experienced a beautiful irony: my successor as president had also started his time there as a janitor.

When I became president, Benson Karanja was the janitor. His optimism, humility, dedication, and intelligence impressed me in every interaction. I promoted him from janitor to library assistant, to head librarian, to accountant as one of our administrators, to professor, to director of student affairs, to vice president, to executive vice president, and finally, to president of the college. During these stages, he studied hard and received multiple degrees.

Throughout this incredible journey, Benson was eager to assume more responsibility, but he always asked penetrating questions about a new role before accepting it. In countless meetings, when I asked him for information, he often told me, "Dr. Chand, I'll look into this and have a report for you in our next meeting." His gracious attitude convinced everyone that he wasn't angling for the next step up the ladder. In each role, he served gladly and tirelessly, affirming and encouraging others around him. As the rest of us watched him, we were inspired to serve gladly and tirelessly, too. Naming him the president of the college was one of the easiest decisions of my career.

From the beginning, I observed Benson's powerfully positive impact on others. It didn't take long to develop a glowing opinion of him; over the years, this opinion grew even stronger. At every turn, I looked for opportunities for him to have a broader, deeper impact on the faculty, staff, and students. I opened a lot of doors for him because he earned my trust and confidence.

I love to open doors for people. In my role now as a culture consultant for a wide variety of organizations, I have more invitations for consulting and speaking than I can accept. Instead of just saying, "No, I can't. I'm very sorry," I tell the person, "I can't, but I know someone who will do an outstanding job for you." I can't walk through the open door, but I can give the opportunity to someone else. My vision statement is short and simple: "Helping others succeed." It's my goal, my heart, and my privilege to open doors for people. That's why I get up every morning.

ALL OF US CAN OFFER OPPORTUNITIES

We don't have to be top leaders to give people opportunities. Of course, if a person has a high position in an organization, she has access to a wider range of ways to promote people who have proven themselves. But all of us—leaders, co-workers, parents, and friends—have the privilege of pointing people to something more meaningful. I'm afraid too many of us take these relationships for granted, so we don't even observe other people very well.

All of us—leaders, co-workers, parents, and friends—have the privilege of pointing people to something more meaningful.

If we'll open our eyes and notice a person's character and talents, we can name them—"I've watched you care for that person and I'm really impressed with your heart," or "You're really talented at…"—and then cast a vision of the future: "I can see you doing… You may not go in that direction, but it's something you can consider because you have what it takes."

I assure you that simple statements like these can make a difference, but only if they are targeted and sincere. In his book, *Extraordinary Influence*, organizational psychologist Tim Irwin distinguishes between two opposite messages: *words of death* and *words of life*.[25]

Words of death undermine a person's safety and confidence, often using criticism to control the person's behavior. These words don't have to be vulgar, loud, or obviously abusive. They can be subtle messages that say, "You don't measure up." These act like sandpaper, gradually eroding the person's sense of value, making him desperate to try harder to prove himself. For this reason, it's effective…in a way. This communication strategy may achieve a short-term gain in performance, but it creates long-term losses because it makes the recipient defensive and angry. In many cases, words of death take the form of blame. The speaker doesn't want to take responsibility for a problem, so he casts a shadow on someone—anyone! And it's usually someone

25. Dr. Tim Irwin, *Extraordinary Influence: How Great Leaders Bring Out the Best in Others* (Hoboken, NJ: John Wiley & Sons, 2018).

who doesn't or can't fight back, someone who plays the role of a scapegoat.

Irwin asserts that *words of life* have restorative power. A simple compliment is nice, but the messages that change lives focus on character, not something superficial. These words, of course, require us to take the time to observe, consider, and reflect on what we see so that our opinion of the person's present and future inspires the heart.

In an interview with *Forbes*, Irwin said:

The word affirmation originates from the Latin *affirmationem*, which means to make steady, to confirm and to strengthen. The deepest form of affirmation strengthens our core—our very sense of self. Brain research strongly supports the dramatic benefits of deep affirmation. Affirmation helps people feel more optimistic and work more productively.[26]

Affirming a person's competence is important, but we can go deeper. Irwin explains:

What is the common thread in Words of Life? These powerful words speak about our character— the unassailability of our inner person. Words of

26. "Performance Feedback: Reach the Heart Through the Brain," Rodger Dean Duncan's interview with Dr. Timothy Irwin about his book, *Extraordinary Influence, Forbes*, April 2, 2018, https://www.forbes.com/sites/rodgerdeanduncan/2018/04/02/performance-feedback-reach-the-heart-through-the-brain/#7276fc725734.

Life address the dimensions of our core and speak the vocabulary of our core, such as integrity, courage, resilience, judgment and authenticity. When spoken authentically, these words can actually transform someone we lead.[27]

If we're self-absorbed, we'll use people to make us feel powerful instead of using our position to help them grow and thrive.

We can easily see that leaders in business and the church can speak this kind of message to others, but sadly, very few do. We can become so absorbed in our own goals and needs that we don't even notice what's going on in the people around us, even in the life of the person sleeping next to us. Some people have the position of being an organizational visionary and they have the privilege of inspiring hope and courage in everyone in the business, church, or non-profit. But all of us have the same privilege to make a powerful impact in the hearts of the people we rub shoulders with each day. To do this, we need someone to speak words of deep affirmation into our lives, so we have a full well to draw

27. Ibid.

from. If we're self-absorbed, we'll *use people* to make us feel powerful instead of *using our position* to help them grow and thrive.

IN THE ORGANIZATIONAL WORLD

The biggest impact we can have on others is through authentic personal connections. However, even narcissistic leaders can provide plenty of opportunities for people in their organizations. The people who are closest to them may suffer from their leader always having to be one-up on everyone, but beyond the executive team, those throughout the rest of the organization can thrive if they have department managers and team leaders who live to help others succeed. For instance, by all accounts, Steve Jobs was a very difficult boss, but he provided incredible opportunities for tens of thousands of people at Apple.

Leaders who don't affirm and inspire those around them produce a low level of engagement from the people on their teams, which inevitably leads to low levels of performance and productivity. The leader's job isn't just to disseminate how-to manuals and keep things on schedule. The first job of leaders is to inspire *hearts*, then to convince *heads*, and only then to give direction to the *hands* of those who actually do the work. When Steve Jobs walked on stage in his black turtleneck and jeans, he inspired his employees with a fresh vision of the future and he explained how new products would revolutionize people's lives. When they walked out of the auditorium, they were eager to play their specific roles in making the revolution in technology come true.

People who work with inspiring leaders and in inspiring environments are sometimes motivated to start their own businesses. Many of the executives at Apple, Facebook, and Microsoft had experiences that gave them confidence to leave and start innovative, successful companies. In my career before January 1, 2004, I received a predictable salary. Organizations paid me to serve as a janitor, youth pastor, pastor, and college president. Since that day, I've had to take responsibility to earn money for my family and the people who work for me without being dependent on any organization. I wouldn't have been able to do this unless I'd been around inspiring leaders and the environments they created. They gave me the courage to step out of the comfortable environment of a predictable income into an uncomfortable environment of an unpredictable income.

The questions I ask myself each day are:

+ Who is farther down the road to success because of my input?

+ Who has more confidence to try something new?

+ Who has a new opportunity that I've helped them see?

The law of sowing and reaping works here: We reap *what* we sow, we reap *after* we sow, and we reap *more than* we sow. When we sow opportunities for others, we'll get many opportunities for ourselves.

In an article for the Association for Talent Development, Bill Treasurer recounts a conversation with his preschool son, Ian. The little boy came home from school one day and with excitement in his voice, he said, "Guess what, Daddy? I got to be the class leader today!"

Treasurer wondered what in the world the class leader in preschool would do. He said, "Really? Class leader? That's a big deal, little buddy. What did you get to do as the class leader?"

Ian answered, "I got to open doors for people!"

Treasurer reflects:

In a matter of fifteen seconds, with seven simple words, Ian clarified what's most important about leadership: creating opportunities for the people you lead. Leaders are simply creators of opportunity for others: They open doors. Think, for example, about a leader whom you greatly admire. Pick someone who has actually led you, versus someone on the world stage. What do you admire about him or her? Did he provide you with an opportunity where you could grow your skills, such as asking you to lead a high-profile project? Did she give you candid feedback that caused you to see yourself in a more honest way? Did he value your perspective, input, and ideas? Didn't the leader you admire create opportunities for you to stretch, grow, and excel?[28]

BLAME AND CREDIT

As we interact with the people we lead, where does the spotlight shine? It's natural for leaders to get a lot of credit for success—and a disproportionate share of the blame when things don't go well—but the best leaders make sure to share the spotlight with others.

As we interact with the people we lead,
where does the spotlight shine?

In fact, the failure to take responsibility for failure and the failure to recognize the contributions of others are two of the most serious leadership flaws. When we point fingers instead of accepting responsibility, we create resentment, but when we shoulder the lion's share of the problem, we gain respect from those on our teams.

28 "Leaders Create Opportunity," Bill Treasurer, Association for Talent Development, April 23, 2013, https://www.td.org/insights/leaders-create-opportunity.

Today, blaming others has become the national sport. In every aspect of life, we're quick to point to others as the cause of our failures. In *A Nation of Victims: The Decay of the American Character*, Charles Sykes says people now sue each other at a far higher rate than ever before. We use the courts to get revenge and get what we want, but the problem goes much deeper than litigation. Sykes describes the entrenchment of believing we've been victimized:

> Victimspeak is the trigger that permits the unleashing of an emotional and self-righteous response to any perceived slight. Charges of racism and sexism continue to be the nuclear weapons of debate, used to shout down nuanced approaches to complex issues. Victimspeak insists upon moral superiority and moral absolutism and thus tends to put an abrupt end to conversation; the threat of its deployment is usually enough to keep others from even considering raising a controversial subject. Ironically, this style of linguistic bullying often parades under the banner of "sensitivity."[29]

Sykes' book was published in 1993 and we've gone farther downhill since then. People on teams in businesses and churches seldom sue one another, but the spirit of blame-shifting is powerful. Far too often, leaders react to

29. Charles J. Sykes, *A Nation of Victims: The Decay of the American Character* (New York: St. Martin's Press, 1993), 16.

mistakes as if they've just witnessed some of the catastrophes in Revelation! In an article for *Inc.* entitled "The 1 Thing Greater Leaders Don't Do," Ron Gibori describes the problem with these leaders and he offers a remedy:

> A common error is assuming that once a mistake has been committed, or revealed, that it is the end of the line. Work often screeches to a halt while the extent of the mistake is exposed, and the culprit brought to justice. All hands are called to the pumps in order to craft a solution in secret, away from judging eyes.
>
> This unfortunate habit leaders have picked up instills a natural fear of mistakes in everyone. Mistakes should not be feared, but expected, and often encouraged. They should be used as an opportunity to teach team members, new employees, interns, and managers.[30]

How do you and I respond to the mistakes of those who report to us? Do we shame them, avoid the issue, and make sure everyone knows it's not our fault? Or do we address the problem honestly, but frame it as an opportunity for growth for the person, for ourselves, and for our organization?

---

30. "The 1 Thing Greater Leaders Don't Do," Ron Gibori, *Inc.*, October 2, 2017, https://www.inc.com/ron-gibori/great-leaders-take-blame-pass-along-credit.html.

Blame is a poison that tastes good on the lips, but kills motivation, ruins relationships, and blocks creativity.

Blame is a poison that tastes good on the lips, but kills motivation, ruins relationships, and blocks creativity.

TEACH PEOPLE TO LOOK FOR OPPORTUNITIES

One of the greatest gifts we can give others is the ability to see opportunities. In my interactions with people at all levels of organizations, I've noticed that many people don't see the open doors right in front of them. We can show them the door of opportunity, or we can do one better and develop them to *notice* open doors long after we've left the scene.

Let me offer these suggestions for leaders who want to help their people see more opportunities:

Teach Them to Observe Others Who Are Moving Forward

What is it about the person who seems to have more advantages than others? It's often that she has become a student of success, preparing for each meeting, helping others succeed, and adding value to the people on her team. It's easy to resent people who are "ladder climbers," but they may not have ulterior motives at all—they may just see opportunities others didn't see. We can train people to notice the characteristics of those who are growing in their skills and advancing in their careers.

Teach Them to Value and Articulate Their Contributions

The goal of writing a good resume is to present yourself as a competent person. This goal shouldn't end on the first day of employment. People who take advantage of opportunities are usually those who have taken the time to understand their unique contribution to the success of the team and the company. This isn't narcissism or boasting; it's simply being aware of their marketability.

Teach Them to Think Broadly and Specifically

Daydreaming is only a bad habit if our people use it for escape. If they daydream about possibilities, it can stimulate creative options, inspire vision, and provide courage to take a bold step into the future. Encourage people on your team to dream big dreams. Their initial concepts may be unrealistic, but plenty of ideas that seemed unrealistic have become realities because someone had the tenacity to fine-tune them and act. Big ideas eventually need to become detailed plans, but not too soon or too late. At the right time, help the person refine the ideas into something that can work.

Teach Them the Importance of Incremental Steps

Quantum leaps in career opportunities seldom happen. Far more often, people climb one step at a time. Gradually, small gains add up and people find they're farther along than they imagined. I've known some people who waited until *the big one* came along…but it never did. They missed a lot of chances to advance in their careers.

Brenda entered the workforce when I became president of the college. She joined a company at a lower level and she was eager to earn a promotion. She was an exemplary employee. After she finished her responsibilities each day, she volunteered to help the manager at the next level—a person who felt overwhelmed by the job. When a role at the next level opened, Brenda was already familiar with the responsibilities and well qualified. She had been intentional about climbing the ladder. She was observed by those above her, they formed a good opinion of her and her skills, and when the door opened, she easily walked through it. As a result of the reputation she earned as a pleasant and tenacious worker, Brenda received several more promotions during her tenure with the company. She achieved her eventual role by taking incremental steps.

Teach Them to Make Themselves Indispensable

When people have confidence in their ability to contribute, they look for jobs for which they are well-suited.

When a task is proposed that can showcase their talents, they volunteer. When no one else is willing to serve in obscurity, they speak up and offer to take the responsibility. They'll find that their supervisor notices and is impressed with their heart and skills.

Teach Them that Sometimes, It's Right to Jump

Some people are impulsive and too optimistic, while others are shackled by *analysis paralysis* and thus too pessimistic. As leaders, we can help our people slow down, do their due diligence, and make a decision to stay or go. We can teach them that there are no guarantees, but sometimes, it's the right thing to jump. When they walk through the new door, most people are surprised by at least some aspect of their new role. That's entirely normal and it's part of life's adventure.

SERVE AS A LAUNCHING PAD

Of course, some leaders don't want to teach their people to take advantage of opportunities. Turnover in organizations can be disruptive and insecure leaders would rather keep the status quo.

But the best leaders see themselves as launching pads for their people, eager to fuel their passion for effectiveness, glad to give direction, and excited about propelling them to a new destination. These leaders create a dynamic, engaged culture—one that attracts the brightest and best to take the places of those who leave.

Our job is to put people in the position to succeed.
If they excel, we have excelled as leaders.

THE RIGHT OPPORTUNITIES

Our job is to put people in the position to succeed. If they excel, we have excelled as leaders. It's imperative that we observe carefully and form accurate opinions of each person's potential. When we put the right people in the right roles, incredible things happen:

Increased Talent Retention

If we match the person's talents, heart, age, and stage in life with a job and provide enough resources, they'll love what they do when they come to work each day. One of the biggest challenges in churches and businesses today is keeping their best people. Yes, it's good to be a launching pad for someone's career, but we can also launch them to a higher trajectory in our own organizations. The question we need to ask when people walk out the door is: why? When people leave because they feel inspired and resourced, we can celebrate. But if our employee churn rate is high, it may be a sign of an unhealthy culture. In an article about employee turnover, the HR resources site Newton explains:

> For most companies, the goal is to hire as many "perfect" candidates as possible, foster a productive and creative workgroup, and keep everyone happy so they stick around for the long run. Companies with a high turnover rate typically get all of these elements wrong and are subjected to damaging consequences such as decreased productivity, high recruitment costs and poor company morale.
>
> A healthy turnover rate will vary from company to company, but essentially, a turnover rate can be considered "healthy" so long as the company can maintain both growth and productivity on an annual basis. To gauge the health of your company, compare your average turnover rate to that of the industry you operate in. This will help you decide whether you are on track or need to take steps towards improvement.[31]

Enthusiasm and Tenacity

When people feel believed in and challenged to do something that makes a difference in the lives of others, they almost always have those tandem qualities that make

31. "Employee Turnover—Reducing Churn in your Company," Newton, https://newtonsoftware.com/blog/2018/05/09/reducing-employee-turnover.

them outstanding employees: *enthusiasm* and *tenacity* to work through every obstacle to get the job done.

People have different engines to their motivation, so it's the leader's job to *look under the hood* to discover what brings out the best in each person. There's always something that drives people to do what they didn't think they could do.

I like to use this illustration: imagine you and me standing on opposite sides of a deep ditch that's filled with all kinds of rotting, disgusting, stinking filth. I open my wallet and say, "If you'll cross through the ditch, I'll give you five dollars." Your response will be immediate and unquestioned: "No thanks!" But if I open a briefcase and offer you $1 million for crossing through the mess, you won't hesitate one second!

When I use this illustration with an audience, I ask a series of questions:

"Did anything change about the distance across the ditch?"

"No," they respond.

"Did anything change about the filth in the ditch?"

"No."

"Did anything change about you?"

"No."

"Did anything change about me?"

"No."

"Then what changed?"

"The motivation to move!"

As students of the people on our teams, we need to find the thing that propels each person to joyfully do their very best. When people are convinced they have greater opportunity on the other side of difficulties, they'll overcome every obstacle.

When passion and talent fit responsibility, people eliminate distractions, secure needed support, find resources, and get more done in less time.

Increased Production

When passion and talent fit responsibility, people eliminate distractions, secure needed support, find resources, and get more done in less time. Of course, there are many motivations for success, including money, titles, comfort, and prestige. However, I've noticed that people in every field long to do something every day that improves the lives of others.

Inspired Teamwork

Two factors are essential for a healthy team: emotional safety and job fulfillment. If these aren't present, you have a collection of individuals, not a team. Emotional safety is the result of clear communication, sharing the spotlight, listening, and the willingness of the leader to take responsibility for his mistakes. When each person feels fulfilled in a job, the team experiences less conflict, turf wars are uncommon, and people generally want each other to succeed.

It's not enough for only one or a few people to be round pegs in round holes. When only a few people fit their roles, the many resent the few—and it's ugly. On some teams, there are a couple of stars and the rest are water-carriers.

Don't let that happen. Make sure each person is in a role that is the best possible fit. Thoughtful placement takes time on the front end, but it saves a lot of heartache on the back end. When people feel safe and fulfilled, they're *engaged* in their work and with the people on their team, they're *energized* to do their best, and they're *excited* to contribute to the team's success.

A Culture of Accountability

When people know they're being observed and the people around them are forming opinions of them, they want to do their best—not out of fear but to contribute. They don't want to let the others down, they want to create products and services that make a difference, and they want to take a step through the next door of opportunity to advance the company, the team, and their careers.

MAKING A DIFFERENCE

We have incredible power to affect the lives of the people around us. We may not realize it, but our interactions build up or tear down, inspire or depress, produce confidence or arouse fear, and open or close doors of opportunity.

When we open doors for others, we're filled with joy because we've made a difference and, quite often, a *big* difference in their lives. As leaders, we're only successful when everyone on our team has the right job fit, sees opportunities for advancement, enjoys their work and each other, and celebrates as much at others' success as at their own.

A very effective leader multiplies himself throughout the leadership team; together, they open doors for others in the organization. When I meet with teams, I look for a "bragging culture." This happens when people brag about each other's accomplishments and contributions instead of their own. That's when you know you have an inspiring culture where people believe the best *in* each other and give their best *for* each other.

Think About It:

+ Who is doing better because of your influence? Whose trajectory is higher because you believed in them?

+ Who feels safe and fulfilled on your team and who shows signs of fear and defensiveness?

+ What would it take to create a "bragging culture" on your team?

Success is where preparation and opportunity meet.
                                            —Bobby Unser,
                    nine-time winner of the Indianapolis 500

CONCLUSION
Continuous Improvement

Most industries implement continual improvement processes that keep "the focus on improving the way things are done on a regular basis. This could be through regular incremental improvements or by focusing on achieving larger process improvements."[32] Some of us are amazingly perceptive about people. We notice little things that reveal a person's heart. A few of us are (let me be kind here) a bit dense and we don't discern what's going on in others' lives unless they're jumping for joy or on the ground bleeding. In my case, I wouldn't be as attentive to creative introverts if I

---

32. "Focusing on Continuous Improvement in the Workplace," Creative Supply, May 3, 2017, https://www.creativesafetysupply.com/articles/continuous-improvement.

hadn't taken the time to learn from them. I've had the best teacher for this lesson: my wife, Brenda.

The vast majority of us are somewhere in between. We have some observational skills, but these certainly can be improved. As our observations become more astute, our opinions of people will be more accurate and we can tailor our communication appropriately about the next steps of opportunity.

FOR ONE WEEK...

All of us can improve. None of us has arrived. We can hone the skill of observation so that we become more perceptive and effective in all of our relationships. It all starts with opening our eyes and ears to notice the words, expressions, and body language of the people around us. Far too often, we're preoccupied with our own agendas, so observing others isn't even on our radars.

Honing the skill of observation starts with noticing the words, expressions, and body language of those around us.

Let me offer a few very specific recommendations for improvement:

+ During the next week, before every meeting or personal interaction, at work or at home, remind yourself to be observant about the person who will be in front of you. If you're spiritually inclined, before these conversations you can pray, "Lord, give me eyes to see, hears to hear, and a heart to care." This simple step will probably take you miles down the road of noticing far more than before.

+ Ask appropriate but personal questions. Even in the corporate or church cultures, as you talk about plans and events, you can ask the person or the group, "What do you think about this idea?" With family and friends, you can ask, "How do you feel about that?" "What would you like to see happen?" "What's meaningful to you about that?"

+ After asking questions, listen. This seems obvious, but many of us are thinking about what we want to say as the person is responding to our question. Do you think they can tell if we're not listening? You bet they can! If we're listening, we have eye contact, we don't rush people to answer, and we value their opinion even if we disagree.

+ Ask follow-up questions. The best way to let people know that we care about them is to ask second and third questions to invite them to express their ideas and their hearts more fully. When we do this, people feel understood, the bedrock of any good relationship.

+ Use the golden statement: "Tell me more about that." Quite often, we don't have to formulate specific follow-up questions. It's even more effective to invite people to give a more expansive answer. This tells them that we really care and it tells us what's really going on in their minds and hearts—and that's what observation is all about.

If you follow these recommendations for a week, you'll almost certainly take major strides to be more observant. Even those who are gifted and shrewd observers will profit and the rest of us may make quantum leaps forward.

In my role as a consultant and in your role as a leader, spouse, parent, or friend, we can become more proficient in five consecutive abilities:

+ *Assess* the person and the situation
+ *Articulate* the challenge and the opportunity
+ *Align* people and resources,
+ Help the person *advance* by identifying the open door
+ Create an encouraging, *accountable* relationship that stimulates continuous progress

As you think about each person on your team or in your family, use this template to consider how you can lead more effectively.

THE MOST IMPORTANT OBSERVATION

The strength of our faith is based on our opinion of God and this opinion is rooted in what we observe about Him. Many books have been written about how our view of God is formed, primarily by our parents and our culture.

For instance, in a consumer culture, many see God as an *especially attentive waiter* who lives only to meet their needs. Others see Him as distant, disengaged, and distracted from what's going on in their lives. And many people think of God as a harsh teacher, a drill sergeant, or a stern judge who's waiting for them to make a mistake so He can blast them with guilt.

The Scriptures invite us to make very different observations and the Gospels give us the clearest account of the character and nature of God. Several decades ago, Harvard professor Henry J. Cadbury (1883–1974) asked his undergraduate students to share their reactions to Jesus. One wrote:

> No one…has yet discovered the word Jesus ought to have said, none suggested the better word he might have said. No action of his has shocked our moral sense. None has fallen short of the ideal. He is full of surprises, but they are all the surprises of perfection. You are never amazed one day by his greatness the next by his littleness. You are quite amazed

that he is incomparably better than you could have expected. He is tender without being weak, strong without being coarse, holy without being servile. He has conviction without intolerance, enthusiasm without fanaticism, holiness without Pharisaism, passion without prejudice. This man alone never made a false step, never struck a jarring note. His life alone moved on those high levels where local limitations are transcended and the absolute Law of Moral Beauty prevails. It was life at its highest.[33]

When Jesus came to Jerusalem for his last week, some Greeks had come to celebrate Passover. They had heard reports about Jesus and they wanted to see Him to take a closer look. They were outsiders, but it didn't matter. They asked Philip for a favor: *"Sir,"* *they said,* *"we would like to see Jesus"* (John 12:21). Philip found Andrew and the two of them asked Jesus to meet with the Greeks. After He spoke with them, a voice from heaven also spoke to the crowd that had gathered there. (See John 12:28).

Isn't that what we want? Isn't that what we need? To see Jesus, to recognize His infinite love combined with limitless power? As our eyes are opened to see Him more as He really is, we change from the inside out. This is the most important observation in our lives and we need to get it right.

---

33. John H. Gerstner, *Reasons for Faith* (New York: Harper & Brothers, 1960), 80; (https://archive.org/details/reasonsforfaith012962mbp/page/n5).

THE POWER OF A TAP

In 1974, when I was a student and had only been in America a short while, I was attending a church near our college. I always sat in the back, but the pastor, Tom Grinder, noticed me. Before each service, he stood in the foyer until the last minute. He may have been greeting people who were barely making it on time, or he may have been praying. At the exact moment the service was scheduled to start, he came through the doors and walked down the aisle to the platform to welcome people. At a midweek service on a Thursday evening, as I sat peacefully on the back row, Pastor Grinder opened the door, but he stopped as soon as he came in. He tapped me on the shoulder, looked into my eyes, and said, "Sam, today you're going to lead the singing." He didn't wait for my response. He just turned and walked quickly down the aisle.

I would have objected. I would have argued with him. At least I would have said, "Let me pray about it." I would have found a way to keep hiding on the back row...but he didn't give me any of those options. I got up and walked to the front of the church. After he greeted the crowd, he said, "Sam Chand is leading our singing tonight." That was my cue. I only knew a few songs. I quickly found them in the songbook and I led the congregation in singing.

I have no idea what prompted Pastor Grinder to tap me on the shoulder. He had never heard me sing; in fact, *I'd* never heard me sing. I'm sure it was a risk for him to ask me to lead that night and I'd give a lot of money to have a video of my performance. (I'd pay for it so I could destroy it!) It was the first time someone asked me to take any leadership role, the first time someone believed in me, the first door that opened for me to have an impact on people. He had observed enough about me to form an opinion that I needed an opportunity. Becoming the song leader was probably the last role I could have imagined, but Pastor Grinder was willing to take the chance. It all began with a tap on my shoulder.

You are where you are today because someone observed something that gave him a good opinion of you and that person opened a door of opportunity for you. It has happened dozens of times and it will continue to happen until you meet Jesus face to face.

Someone out there holds the key to your future.

You have the responsibility and privilege of playing that role in the lives of others. If you take the time to observe, your considered opinion will give you wisdom to open the right doors for them.

You hold the key to many people's futures.

THE BEAUTY OF GRATITUDE

From time to time, we need to stop our busy lifestyles and reflect on the question at the beginning of this book: "How did I get here?" Yes, we've experienced setbacks and heartaches, but we're at this point in our lives, with these people, in this role, because other people saw something in us that impressed them enough to tap us on the shoulder and invite us to take a step forward. When I think of the people who have done this for me, I forget about the nagging list of things I need to do and I marvel that these people cared enough to open those doors.

Set aside your nagging to-do list and take time to be grateful for the people who cared enough to open doors for you.

The Roman philosopher, statesman, and orator Cicero said, "Gratitude is not only the greatest of virtues, but the parent of all the others." I'm very thankful for the people who stood up for me when I was down and saw a better future for me when no one else saw my potential. I'm grateful for those who have told others that I've helped them in some way. All of these people form a ladder of success for me and have inspired me to live in a way that has an impact on others.

I'm sure you can identify the people who have done this for you. Where would you be if they hadn't played such important roles in your life?

Think About It:

+ Are you willing to implement the suggestions to improve your observational skills over the next week? If you are, what do you expect to happen?

+ Describe the importance of having a more accurate observation of Jesus.

+ Where would you be today if particular people hadn't observed you, formed positive opinions of you, and opened doors of opportunity?

+ Take some time to thank God for them.

+ What are three principles or practices in this book that you are committed to implement? What difference will they make?

If you can dream it, then you can achieve it. You will get all you want in life if you help enough other people get what they want.   —Zig Ziglar

ABOUT THE AUTHOR

Sam Chand's singular vision for his life is to help others succeed. A prolific author and renowned international consultant, he speaks regularly at leadership conferences, corporations, business roundtables, seminars, and other leadership development opportunities.

Being raised in a pastor's home in India has uniquely equipped Sam to share his passion to mentor, develop, and inspire leaders to break all limits. He has been called a dream releaser, leadership architect, and change strategist.

In the 1970s, as a student at Beulah Heights College, Sam served as a janitor, cook, and dishwasher to finance his education. He returned in 1989 as president—and under his leadership, Beulah Heights University became the country's largest predominantly African-American Christian college.

Sam holds an honorary Doctor of Humane Letters from Beulah Heights University, an honorary Doctor of Divinity from Heritage Bible College, a Master of Arts in Biblical Counseling from Grace Theological Seminary, and a Bachelor of Arts in Biblical Education from Beulah Heights. He has mentored leaders in churches and ministries as well as international corporations and business start-ups. He was named one of the top thirty global leadership gurus by www.leadershipgurus.net.

Sam has authored more than a dozen books on leadership, including *New Thinking, New Future*; *Culture Catalyst*; *Bigger Faster Leadership*; *Leadership Pain*; *Who's Holding Your Ladder?*; *What's Shakin' Your Ladder?*; and *12 Success Factors of an Organization*.

For more information or to connect with Sam, please visit www.samchand.com.

RECEIVE **FREE LEADERSHIP** TRAINING IN YOUR INBOX EVERY TUESDAY!

In these videos, I share a 2-3 minute nugget that will enhance your leadership.

Sign up for free! www.samchand.com

OTHER BOOKS BY SAM CHAND

NEW THINKING, NEW FUTURE

The way leaders think matters—it matters a lot. The problem is that we almost universally make a colossal subconscious assumption that the way we think is the only possible way to consider our situations...We need to upgrade the software in our heads!

CULTURE CATALYST

Often, organizational leaders confuse culture with vision and strategy, but they are very different. Vision and strategy usually focus on products, services, and outcomes, but culture is about the people—an organization's most valuable asset.

BIGGER, FASTER LEADERSHIP

More passion isn't the answer, and bigger dreams aren't always the solution. Every leader is asking two questions: How can we grow? How can we grow faster? The only way organizations can grow bigger and move faster is by accelerating the excellence of their systems and structures.

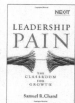

LEADERSHIP PAIN

Do you want to be a better leader? Raise the threshold of your pain. Do you want your church to grow or your business to reach higher goals? Reluctance to face pain is your greatest limitation. There is no growth without change, no change without loss, and no loss without pain.

AVAILABLE ON AMAZON OR ANYWHERE BOOKS ARE SOLD

GET FREE ACCESS TO MODULE ONE

OF THE *SAM CHAND LEADERSHIP INSTITUTE!*

The **Sam Chand Leadership Institute** is a virtual environment where high-performing leaders gather to create success, grow their network, and expand their capacity for more.

SAMCHANDLEADERSHIP.COM/SPECIAL

AVAIL

The ART *of* LEADERSHIP

GET A FREE
ONE-YEAR SUBSCRIPTION
TO OUR MAGAZINE

WWW.AVAILLEADERSHIP.ORG/FREE

Welcome to Our House!

We Have a Special Gift for You

It is our privilege and pleasure to share in your love of Christian books. We are committed to bringing you authors and books that feed, challenge, and enrich your faith.

To show our appreciation, we invite you to sign up to receive a specially selected **Reader Appreciation Gift**, with our compliments. Just go to the Web address at the bottom of this page.

God bless you as you seek a deeper walk with Him!

WE HAVE A GIFT FOR YOU. VISIT:

whpub.me/nonfictionthx

WHITAKER
HOUSE